AF450539

China's New Diplomacy Concept: Building a Community of Shared Future for Mankind

Chen Yue & Pu Ping

CANUT INTERNATIONAL PUBLISHERS

Istanbul -Berlin -London -Santiago -Cape Town

This book is published in cooperation with China Renmin University Press (CRUP) in Beijing
Proofread by Wang Jianping & translated by Nie Yunping

Chinese Title: 构建人类命运共同体
Copyright © China Renmin University Press, Beijing, 2017

Canut International Publishers
Canut Intl. Turkey, Batı Mh. Karanfil Sk. 10/5, Pendik , Istanbul, Turkey
Canut Intl. Germany, Heerstr. 266, D-47053, Duisburg, Germany
Canut Intl. United Kingdom, 12a Guernsay Road, London E11 4BJ, England
Copyright © Canut International Publishers, 2021

ISBN: 978-605-7693-51-8
Also available as e-book

www.canutbooks.com

About the Author

Chen Yue, born in 1956, is the dean, professor and doctoral supervisor of the School of International Relations, Renmin University of China. He is currently the dean of the National Security Research Institute of Renmin University of China, a member of the Degree Evaluation Committee of Renmin University of China, and the chairman of the Political Science and Sociology Branch of Renmin University of China. Concurrently serves as the chairman of the National University International Politics Research Association, the deputy director of the Political Science Steering Committee of the Ministry of Education, a special director of the Contemporary World Research Center, a member of the editorial board of "Politics Studies" magazine, academic consultant of "International Political Studies" magazine, and "Diplomatic Review" "Magazine consultant".

Pu Ping, a professor at the School of International Relations, Renmin University of China. Mainly engaged in teaching and research in the fields of China's multilateral diplomacy, international organizations, and international law. Published academic monographs "International Organizations in the Contemporary World", "China's Peaceful Development and International Institutions", participated in the writing of "Contemporary World Economy and Politics", "International Organizations" and other textbooks, and published in "Teaching and Research" and "International Forum". Dozens of papers have been published in journals.

Contents

Preface

The Intrinsic Relation Between China's Global Diplomacy and Domestic Governance: Xi Jinping's New Visions

In the past three decades since China implemented the policy of reform and opening up to the outside world, China has entered a brand new period of development. By 2010, China's economic aggregate has surpassed Japan as the second largest economy in the world. China has entered a period of all-round in-depth reform, a period that is at once marked by a number of new characteristics and full of great contradictions and strategic opportunities. The period of "New Normal", which appeared as a result of decades of high economic growth, proves to be a catalyst for the transition and upgrading of economic structure and radical shift of economic development mode. As a result, China has crossed the "middle income trap" and is quickly moving towards the ranks of moderately developed countries. In political construction, with the top-level design of the Communist Party and its unique model of political development, its institutional regulations and rules will become more mature and solid by 2020, its style and method of governance more scientific and democratic, ushering a new phase of modernization of state governance. In cultural construction, further reform of the cultural system will be pushed ahead, with the core socialist values more deeply rooted and China's cultural soft power globally extended. In the field of social construction, the goal is to complete the process of building a moderately well-off society in all aspects by 2020, when society will be more harmonious and people's life will be improved. With respect to building an eco-civilization, the system of ecological civilization will be more perfect, and the construction of a beautiful China will be more fruitful. In the international context, the impact of the global financial crisis has not ended, and the world order is undergoing extensive and profound changes. The world order, dominated by the West for the past three hundred years, is now on the decline.

With these rapid changes occurring in domestic and world situation, we have entered an era that is badly in need of theories and full of potential for generating new ones, an era in urgent need of innovative thought and capable of generating new ideas. It is against such background, since the Eighteenth National Congress of the CPC, that the Party Central Committee under the leadership of comrade Xi Jinping at the core has carried out theoretical innovation on the basis of practice, and proposed a set of new concepts, new ideas and new strategies concerning the governance of China, constituting Xi Jinping's thought for running the country.

1. The Formation of Xi Jinping's Thought on the Governance of China

Since the 18th National Congress of the Chinese Communist Party, in the great practice of further building socialism with Chinese characteristics, Xi Jinping has deepened the understanding of the ruling law of the Communist Party, laws for building socialism, laws of the development of human society, by putting forward a series of new concepts, ideas and strategies for managing China's reform and development stability, internal affairs, foreign affairs and national defense, as well as governing the Party, state and army. Xi's theory of statecraft, gradually formed over the past years, is rich in content, complete in system, deep in thought and logic. This system of thought will serve as the guiding principle for the new historical period, for deepening reform in a comprehensive way, expanding the scope of its opened-up areas, speeding up socialist modernization process, and realizing the goal of the great rejuvenation of the Chinese nation.

Briefly, the main content of Xi Jinping's thought on the governance of China include "realizing the Chinese dream of the Great Revival," upholding and developing "socialism with Chinese characteristics," adhering to the principle of "People Centered" value orientation, a new concept of development based upon "Five Major Ideas" as its main focus, "Four Comprehensives" strategic layout, the theory of economic development based upon "supply-side structural reform" as the main line, resulting in a national governance theory consisting of national governance system and modernization of governance capability, legal theory for "a comprehensive framework for promoting the rule of law," Party building thought of "comprehensive and strict Party management," "the concept of the overall national security" and the theory of global governance for "human destiny community. "Xi Jinping's theory of state governance consists of several levels, aspects and dimensions. First of all, the theory lays out the blueprint for the goal. the idea and the basic path of the country's development, thus resolving the fundamental problem as to the direction and the route of such development. Secondly, Xi derives the concept of development from value orientation and designs the strategic layout accordingly, thus completing the task of global overall deployment once for all. Lastly, Xi has extended the theory and put forward a series of new ideas concerning economic reform, political, legal, and social construction, cultivation of ecology-based civilization, an all out effort to enforce strict Party discipline, national security and global governance, thus solving the governance problems in key areas. The above-mentioned set of ideas form an organic whole, constituting a scientific ideological and theoretical system.

Xi Jinping's theory of national governance is based upon a senes of scientific thoughts and methods, with Marxist doctrine as guiding principle, which may be summed up as follows: find the law, view the general situation, size up the overall situation, set the key, control the bottom line and co-ordinate.

First, the notion of "find the law" suggests that Xi Jinping is particularly keen on exploring the laws behind the evolution of human society through a historical vision, summarizing past development experience, and pointing out the direction for the future.

Second, "to view the general situation" suggests that Xi Jinping has always been observant of the tide of the times and capable of grasping the potential trend of situations both at home and abroad. In order to correctly assess the situation, we must take advantage of opportunities, strategically confront new situations, resolve unfavorable factors and turn disadvantages into an advantage.

Third, "to size up the overall situation" means that Xi is capable of strategic and systematic thinking, strategizing ultimate solutions to issues of basic, global, long-term, integral significance, thus firmly in control of the whole situation.

Fourth, "to set the key" suggests that Xi is adept at distinguishing major and minor contradictions on the one hand, and the major and minor aspects of these contradictions on the other, finding the key points and seeking correct solutions. All these constitute a theory of thought that can meet the demands of the times.

Fifth, "to control the bottom line," according to Xi, means to be good at "bottom-line thinking." We should always be prepared against the bad and strive for the best, so that the initiative can be firmly grasped. It is imperative that we aim at the problems and challenges, set the minimum goal objectively and strive for the best result.

Lastly, "to coordinate." Xi is good at scientifically coordinating reform tasks, organizing and orchestrating various reform initiatives according to the tasks and measures of heavy and light, anxious and slow, primary and secondary difficulty, and prerequisite conditions.

Xi Jinping's theory of governance integrates the logic of scientific socialism and the historical logic of China's economic and social development. On the one hand, Xi stresses the necessity of adhering to the fundamental principles of scientific socialism, as we should not forget our ancestors, so to speak. Socialism with Chinese characteristics is the Chinese version of scientific socialism, the epitome of five hundred years of international socialism. On the other hand, Xi pays special attention to the inherent historical logic of Chinese social development, suggesting that "we are destined to follow a route of our own, a route suitable for our own characteristics because of our singular cultural tradition, unique historical destiny and the particular fundamental conditions of the nation. "In this way, theoretical self-confidence, institutional self-confidence and cultural self-confidence will be increased.

Furthermore, Xi's theory of state governance embodies the unity of theoretical inheritance and theoretical innovation. It answers a series of important theoretical and practical questions concerning the development of the Party and the state under the new circumstances, thus carrying on the best of the Chinese cultural heritage and at the same time closely integrating with the current world situation and China's development practice. The set of new concepts, new ideas and new strategies aim to maintain and inherit the practical experience, theoretical achievements, glorious tradition and the Party's fine style of work. Xi's theory of governance of China is imbued with the spirit, outlook, methodology, and the fundamental principles of Marxism. Therefore, Xi's theory of governance has carried forward the tradition of Marxism-Leninism, Mao Zedong Thought, Deng Xiaoping Theory, the important thought of "Three Represents" and the theoretical system of "Scientific Outlook on Development." At the same time, the theory has kept up with the times.

Xi's theory of the governance of China has taken into account the concerns of the present and the experience of the past. Xi has pointed out that adherence to problem-oriented methods is a distinctive feature of Marxism. Xi's art of statecraft embodies such problem-oriented consciousness. In conforming to the trend of the times and grasping the trend of the times, Xi has based his theory upon the historical practice of the Chinese people as well as the advanced experience of various countries in the world, deriving nourishment from China's excellent traditional culture and summing up the new experience created by the Party leading the people. With this set of new ideas, Xi has creatively responded to the new issues of the present times and contemporary China, thus pioneering new ways for the sinicization of Marxism.

Xi's theory of governance of China has combined Chinese perspective and global spirit. It takes an unequivocal Chinese stand, prioritizing the realization of the great rejuvenation of the Chinese nation as its central mission, as it reflects the appeal and desire of the Chinese people. At the same time, Xi's theory attempts at a broad view of the domestic and international situations. This unification of Chinese perspective and global spirit, together with the concept of "building a human community with shared destiny," constitutes Xi's major contribution to and innovation of diplomatic theory and practice.

2. Xi Jinping: The Governance of China

Xi Jinping's theory of the governance of China is a complete scientific theoretical system with rich implications, covering a diverse array of topics such as reform and development, internal affairs, foreign affairs and national defense.

■   **"Realizing the Chinese Dream of the Great Rejuvenation of the Chinese Nation" as the Ultimate Goal of Development**

Ever since the 18th National Congress of CPC, Xi Jinping has envisioned and planned China's future development by reviewing and summarizing the development process of the Chinese nation. Having explained the Party's "Two Centenary Goals" established during the 18th National Congress of CPC, Xi further propounded the objective of "realizing the Chinese dream of the great rejuvenation of the Chinese nation" by explaining and defining the meaning, essence, significance and development requirement of the concept of "Chinese Dream," thus forming a fully expounded theory of "Chinese Dream." Xi points out that rejuvenating the nation has been the greatest dream of the Chinese nation since modern times, a dream that reflects the long-cherished wish of several generations of Chinese people and the overall interests of the Chinese nation and the Chinese people, the common aspiration of every Chinese. The dream of the great rejuvenation has profoundly revealed the historical process of Chinese social development since modern times, concretely reveals the historical mission of the Chinese nation and highlights the grand vision of building socialism with Chinese characteristics.

The essence of the Chinese dream consists in achieving prosperity of the country, rejuvenation of the nation and happiness of the people. In order to realize the dream, we must follow the Chinese road, carry forward the spirit of the Chinese nation and unite all Chinese forces. The road of socialism with Chinese characteristics is the fundamental way to realize the Chinese dream; it is the only way to realize the prosperity of the country, rejuvenation of the nation and happiness of the people. In the long course of the nation's history, the Chinese nation has consolidated a strong national spirit with patriotism at its core. At the same time, in the process of building up the motherland, we have gathered a strong spirit of the times with reform and innovation at the core. The future and destiny of every individual are closely bound up with those of the nation. The Chinese dream cannot do without the effort of millions of people united as one man. We need to rely on the hard work of all the people, upon the unremitting effort from generations of Chinese people.

- **"Adhering to and Advance along the Path of Socialism with Chinese Characteristics"**

Road determines destiny. In order to realize the Chinese dream of national rejuvenation, we should adhere to the basic road of socialism with Chinese characteristics. Since the 18th National Congress of CPC, Xi has put forward a series of important viewpoints and conclusions concerning upholding and developing socialism with Chinese characteristics, which accumulate into a systematic theory of "Adhering to and Developing the Basic Road of Socialism with Chinese Characteristics. "In this way, Xi has responded to the question raised by some about whether socialism with Chinese characteristics is authentic socialism, expounded the road and direction of China's socialist construction and consolidated the ideals and faith in communism."

Since the reform and opening up, some scholars have raised questions concerning the nature of socialism with Chinese characteristics, whether it is authentic socialism, or the right type of socialism. In view of these arguments and queries, Xi Jinping has responded in unequivocal terms: "characteristic socialism is socialism, not any other doctrine." He also suggests, history and reality tell us that only socialism can save China, only socialism with Chinese characteristics can put China on the right track. "This is the conclusion of history, and it is people's choice."

Xi has systematically expounded the need to further develop socialism with Chinese characteristics, particularly the importance of upholding and developing socialism with Chinese characteristics. Whatever policies of reform and opening China will ultimately adopt, we must always adhere to the road of socialism with Chinese characteristics, the theoretical systems and institutions. He has explained clearly the characteristic of socialism with Chinese characteristics. Socialism with Chinese characteristics, he says, is special in the nature of route, theoretical system, institutional structure, as well as in the way it is to be achieved, the guiding principles for action and the inner link of fundamental guarantee. It is special precisely because all three are unified in the great practice of socialism with Chinese characteristics. He strongly urges to make a historical assessment of scientific socialism, to discover something new, something creative, something prophetic, with the ultimate goal of enriching socialism with Chinese characteristics in the fields of practice, theory, nationality, and time. Xi stresses that we should enhance our confidence in choosing the road, theoretical self-confidence, institutional self-confidence and cultural self-confidence. We should eliminate and correct all kinds of wrong ideas and unswervingly adhere to and keep pace with the times to develop socialism with Chinese characteristics.

Xi Jinping's idea of "upholding and developing socialism with Chinese characteristics" establishes the fundamental principles of socialism with Chinese characteristics, which will enable us to confront the complex situations at home and abroad, confirm the ideals of communism, and draw out the path and direction of China's socialist construction.

▪ The Value Orientation of "People as the Center"

Who should benefit from development, and who should own the product of development? These arc the first problems to be solved before a sound notion and strategy of development can ever be established. Since the 18th National Congress of CPC, Xi Jinping has proposed a series of new ideas and propositions such as "people-centered," "people position," "the people's morale," "giving people a sense of gain," etc. These ideas have gradually formed a system of thought on "people as the center," and thus further enriched and developed the socialist outlook on people with Chinese characteristics.

Xi has frequently urged that "we should put into practice the notion of people-centered development. The idea of 'people-centered development' is not an abstract, empty concept, nor is it mere talk and ideology; rather, it should be reflected in all aspects of economic and social development."

The idea of "people's standpoint" is an important component of Xi Jinping thought. Xi pointed out at the 95th anniversary of CPC in Chongqing that "people's standpoint" is the fundamental political position taken by the Chinese Communist Party, which distinguishes the Chinese Communist Party from other parties. The Party and the people stand together through storm and stress, keep flesh and blood together. It is the fundamental guarantee for the Party to overcome all difficulties and risks.

The notion is drawn from the political wisdom of traditional Chinese culture, as shown in such sayings as "people being the foundation of the state" and "whoever wins the hearts of the people rules the world," and then applied to the social reality of China today. This new theory of "people's morale" may be expressed in very concrete terms, as is manifest in the following statements: "people's morale is the biggest politics, and justice is the strongest force"; "Environmental pollution is a high incidence, becoming the livelihood of the people, the pain of the people"; "A peaceful and stable development and prosperity is the common aspiration of the people"; "If the Party wishes to win popular support, the Party Central Committee must be authoritative and must be honest. "In order to win the hearts of the people, Xi Jinping stresses, all our work should ultimately allow people to have a sense of gain.

- **The New Concept of Development with the Core of "Five Principles"**

The concept of development is the forerunner of developmental action; it fundamentally determines the success or failure of development. At the 5th Session of the 18th National Congress of CPC, Xi Jinping systematically discussed the "five principles" of innovation, coordination, green life, openness and sharing. Based upon a profound summary of experience and lessons at home and abroad, and critical analysis of domestic and foreign development theories, the concept of new development reveals the law of economic and social development scientifically and objectively. The concept is an idea of great progress in so far as it has deepened our Party's understanding and grasp of the law of development, enriched and developed the theoretical treasure of socialism with Chinese characteristics.

The solid establishment and effective implementation of the "new concept of development" is an important event in context of China's development, as it relates to the "13th Five-Year" period and even more extensive period of China's development strategy, development mode and development focus. Although China has made remarkable achievements in economic construction, it has also accumulated problems. New concepts of development are needed to solve the problems and guide us further ahead. We should prioritize innovation in the agenda of overall national development, promote theoretical, institutional, scientific and technological innovations, cultural innovation and other aspects of innovation, in order to achieve comprehensive competitiveness through innovative development.

We should grasp the overall layout, deal with major relations, achieve and enhance coordinated development. We will promote sustainable economic and social construction of resource-saving and environment-friendly nature, thus adhering to the idea of green development and the aim of building a beautiful China. We will pursue a win-win strategy of opening up to the outside world, cultivate a higher level of open economy, and promote open development. We will persist in the principle of development for the people, reliance on the people, and sharing the fruits of development by the people. Only through effective institutional arrangements shall we be able to achieve shared development.

▪ The Coordination and Promotion of the "Four-Pronged Comprehensive Strategy"

In order to realize the great rejuvenation of the Chinese nation, we must make strategic plans according to the developmental needs of the situation. Since the 18th National Congress of CPC, Xi Jinping has proposed the "Four-Pronged Comprehensive Strategy," a blueprint for governing the country in the new situation.

The "Four-Pronged Comprehensive Strategy" is an overall strategic layout initiated by the Party Central Committee under Xi's leadership by adhering to and developing the strategic layout of the overall situation of socialism with Chinese characteristics. It is a "road map," so to speak, for realizing the goals of "dual centenaries" and the Chinese dream of national rejuvenation. The implementation of the "Four-Pronged Comprehensive Strategy" shows that the new central collective leadership of the Party has improved the overall strategy of governing the country. It indicates that our Party's understanding of the governing law of the Party, the law of socialist construction and the development of human society has reached a new level. As a result, the Party has taken another important leap in leading the people towards the grand goal.

Xi Jinping points out, "The 'Four-Pronged Comprehensive Strategy' is a strategic layout that includes strategic objective and measures, each one of the four 'comprehensives' in itself possesses strategic significance. "Of the four comprehensives, to finish building a moderately prosperous society constitutes a phase of the strategic goals of the Chinese dream, i.e. realization of socialist modernization and rejuvenation of the Chinese nation. It is to be accomplished directly under the strategic leadership of the Party and the state's development at this stage. Comprehensive deepening of reform is the key to achieve strategic objectives, a fundamental path; comprehensive rule of law is the basic way and reliable guarantee to achieve the strategic objectives; full and strict Party management is the essence of the Party's strong leadership; an all-out effort to enforce strict Party discipline is to give full play to the core role of the Party's strong leadership and providing a strong organizational guarantee for the realization of the strategic objectives. We shall ensure that the four comprehensives be carried out throughout all procedures and all aspects of the things we do, so that they will complement each other, promote each other, contrast with each other, thus gathering more positive momentum to coordinate and promote the "Four-Pronged Comprehensive Strategy."

- **Economic Development Thought with "the Structural Reform of Supply-side" at the Core**

Xi Jinping first proposed the idea of "the structural reform of supply-side" when he was presiding over the Eleventh Meeting of the Leading Group of the Central Finance and Economy. It evolves into a comprehensive system of economic thought of development that covers reform essence, reform priority, reform content, and reform measures. The theory of the structural reform of supply-side showcases the application of the basic methods of Marx doctrine to the political economy of socialism with Chinese characteristics. It is also an enormous breakthrough in the field of macro-economics, and development economic theory and institutional economic analysis in the political economy of socialism with Chinese characteristics. It is nothing less than a systematic revolution of economics in constructing a political economy with Chinese characteristics.

The structural reform of supply-side is a major innovation in understanding, adaptation and leadership. To sustain economic growth, it is imperative that we recognize the new normal, adapt to the new normal, and lead the new normal. The structural reform of supply side has been the most important, far-reaching and systematic economic reform in the new normal period, as well as the most scientific, practical and efficient economic development and reform in the process of China's adapting to the new normal and seizing the new opportunities therein.

In addition, since the 18th National Congress, the Party Central Committee under Xi Jinping's leadership also put forward other important strategic ideas and theories with regard to developing socialist economy with Chinese characteristics. These ideas and theories include centralizing the role of the market in allocating resources and adjusting the role of the government; establishing a basic economic system with the co-existence of public ownership and diversified ownership, with the former as the dominant form; making the state owned enterprises bigger, stronger and better; perfecting the integrative mechanism of urban and rural development, promoting equal exchange of urban and rural factors, rational allocation and equalization of basic public services; speeding up the construction of an open economic new system; promoting higher levels of opening up to the outside world; taking an active part in global economic governance and building a community of common human destiny. These ideas and theories go a long way toward enriching and developing Marxist political economy and the political economy of socialism with Chinese characteristics, thus opening a new era of development for the political economy of socialism with Chinese characteristics.

■ A State Governance Theory that Aims at Modernizing the National Governance System and Governing Capabilities

In the Third Plenary Session of the 18th CPC Central Committee, the Party propounded the overall goal of deepening reform as perfecting and developing the socialist system with Chinese characteristics, modernizing our governance system and governance capabilities. This overall goal represents a deepening and systemization of the understanding of state modernization and reform development by the Party Central Committee under Xi's leadership. It is also a new arrangement for the construction of socialism with Chinese characteristics, an important innovation of the Party's principle of governing state affairs, and an enrichment and development of Marxist theory of the state.

As Xi Jinping points out, national governance system and governance capability represent the system of a country and its capability to implement policies. The system of national governance, with its set of closely linked and coordinated state systems, is the system of managing the state under the leadership of the Party. The capacity of state governance is the ability to use the state system to manage all aspects of society. The national governance system and governance capability form a complementary organic whole. Only with good national governance system can we really improve governance and give full play to the effectiveness of the national governance system. As the core of the governance system, the role of the system is basic, thorough and long-term. Without effective governance, however, no system can ever hope to function.

According to Xi Jinping, we shall quicken the modernization of China's governance system and the improvement of our governance capabilities; we must fully understand and grasp the overall goal of deepening reform in a comprehensive way. The two tasks arc actually complementary, improving and developing socialist system with Chinese characteristics and updating national governance system and governing capability simultaneously. The first task refers to the principle of fundamental direction and basic road, that the direction and road of the national governance system and updating governing capability correspond with the path of socialism with Chinese characteristics. The second task refers to the conditions of realization and ways of construction, i.e., the conditions and ways to practice socialism with Chinese characteristics rely on constantly improving the national governance system and enhancing national governance capabilities.

▪ Legal Thought on "Law-based Governance of China"

Governing the country by law is the essential requirement and important guarantee for adhering to and developing socialism with Chinese characteristics as well as the prerequisite of realizing the modernization of the national governance system and governance capability. Ever since the 18th National Congress of CPC, Xi Jinping has put forward a series of new ideas on the theme of "ruling the country according to law", forming a systematic theory of rich and profound legal thought. The essence of such thinking includes the following: socialism with Chinese characteristics, rule of law, theory of relations between the Party and the law, theory on ruling the country by law, ruling the country according to the constitution and ruling by constitution, the relationship of rule of law and reform, and anti-corruption theory in accordance with the law.

Xi Jinping urges to adhere to the socialist system of laws with Chinese characteristics, which is essentially a manifestation of socialism with Chinese characteristics in the legal field. The socialist system of laws with Chinese characteristics is a product of the theory of socialism with Chinese characteristics on the issue of rule of law. This socialist system of law with Chinese characteristics is the legal form of China's socialist system of law with Chinese characteristics. Xi's theory indicates that the socialist system of law with Chinese characteristics, rule of law theory, and legal system belong to the more general theories of socialist road with Chinese characteristics, theory and system, which is the manifestation of the latter in the field of law and rule of law.

On the relation of the Party and the law, Xi Jinping admonishes, "we should never forget that Party's leadership is the soul of the socialist system of law with Chinese characteristics, which is the major difference between the rule of law in China and that of Western capitalist countries. "Other related new thoughts on the rule of law include the following: Legal construction necessitates governance, management and administration of the country simultaneously through the rule of law. We should uphold the principle of the management of the state, government and society through the rule of law. The life and the authority of law lie in its implementation. Reform ought to be based on legal evidence, whereas legislation should promote reform. We should use the system to manage the power and manage the people, so as to confine the exercise of power within an institutional cage.

- **"Comprehensively Strengthening Party Discipline" and Xi Jinping's Thought on Party Building**

The Party is the key to success whether in upholding and improving the socialist system with Chinese characteristics, or in promoting the modernization of national governance. Since the 18th National Congress, Xi Jinping has always attached great importance to Party building. On several occasions, he stressed that the Party should manage and strictly discipline the Party. He proposed a series of new ideas and measures on Party management, forming a firm, dignified and scientific system of thought on "comprehensive and strict Party management. "The core of these ideas includes ideological Party building, system Party management, strict governance of officials, and strict Party discipline.

The Sixth Plenary Session of the 18th CPC Central Committee has summarized the important achievements made by the Party in comprehensively disciplining the Party, the most important of which is the persistence with which the Central Committee of the Communist Party of China under Xi Jinping's leadership has maintained the integration of ideological Party building with systematic Party building. We are advised to make good use of the legacy of ideological Party building and firmly grasp the key of ideological education. Ideological Party building is the source of Party building, and systematic Party building is the foundation of Party building. By tempering toughness with gentleness, the two measures work effectively. We should implement the overall plan and requirements of strictly disciplining the Party, promote the Party's construction in the spirit of reform. By rule of law and legal practice, we can establish a system of rules, clarify the legal procedures, discipline the Party, so that the system Party building will be followed thoroughly and the general level of Party management will be raised. With the establishment and perfection of the Party system, the leadership of the Party will become more vigorous, efficient and authoritative.

"To strictly discipline the Party, the key is to strictly discipline the officials." The government should strictly select, train and supervise the officials, selecting and using the right people being the bottom line of cadre work. Xi Jinping has reiterated on several occasions that we must strengthen discipline construction, attaching greater importance to maintaining discipline and code of conduct. We should constantly improve Party discipline as the situation and Party building require, and ensure that the system of rules will be properly followed and applied. Party organizations at all levels are thus required to actively explore ways of regular and institutionalized disciplinary education, and always adhere to the discipline and be highly alert to any violation of it, so that discipline will become taboo like electrified wires, so to speak.

▪ Conceptualizing National Security through "Overall National Security Concept"

The notion of overall national security was first proposed by Xi Jinping at the First Session of the National Security Council. The overall National Security Concept was formulated by the Central Committee of the Communist Party of China under Xi Jinping's leadership to confront the new situations, features and problems of national security. It is also an indispensable component of the whole set of new concepts, ideas and strategies on the governance of China propounded by the Party Central Committee. The concept of overall national security came into being in the midst of complicated domestic and international environment in which the construction of socialism with Chinese characteristics occurs. In accordance with traditional Chinese strategic thinking of national security, the concept has innovated and sublimated the tradition of strategic thinking on national security since the founding of New China.

The concept of national security is rich in connotation and denotation, which is best summed up as "Five Major Factors." The "Five Major Factors" include the notion of people's security as the central principle, political security as the goal, economic security as the base, military, cultural and social security as the guarantee, and enhancement of global security as being foundational. "Five Pairs of Relations" include relations of external security vs. internal security, homeland security vs. civilian security, traditional types of security and non-traditional types of security, the issue of development vs. the issue of security, individual security vs. collective security. It covers "eleven important fields" such as political security, homeland security, military, economic, cultural and social security, security of science and technology, cyber and ecological security, resources and nuclear security, etc.

The idea of strengthening the armed forces is part of the overall national security concept. Since the 18th National Congress, in order to better adapt to the new international strategic pattern and national security situation, to build a national defense force and a powerful army commensurate with China's international status and national security interests, the Central Committee of the Communist Party of China under Xi Jinping's leadership has made overall plans for the armed forces to be revolutionary, modernized and regularized, and coordinated economic development and national defense construction. The series of policies and principles, which aim at guiding the reform and innovation of national defense and armed forces, ultimately lead to the formation of important ideological theories which will guide and realize the goal of building a strong army.

- **The Theory of Global Governance on Human Destiny Community**

Since the 18th National Congress of the CPC, Xi Jinping has put forward a series of new ideas such as "the destiny community of the Chinese nation," "Asian destiny community" and community of shared interests, together with a whole new series of ideas, strategies and plans with regard to international relations and global governance, resulting in a systematic theory of global governance which takes the human destiny community as the main line. The core of the theory includes the strategic conception of "The Belt and Road," peripheral diplomatic strategies of "amity, sincerity, mutual benefit and inclusiveness," "the construction of new type of international relations," and adherence to the idea of co-construction and shared governance, etc.

"The Belt and Road" initiative is designed to promote common development and achieve win-win cooperation and common prosperity, as well as to increase mutual understanding and trust, and strengthen peaceful and friendly exchanges in an all-round way. As always, Chinese government will uphold the concept of peaceful cooperation, openness, inclusive, mutual learning and mutual benefit, engage in pragmatic cooperation in all fields and build a political community of mutual trust, economic integration, cultural inclusiveness, a community of destiny and responsibility. With regard to global governance, Xi Jinping suggests that all countries should strengthen communication and coordination and take care of each other's interests and concerns; they should discuss the rules and build a common mechanism to meet the challenges. Global economic governance should aim at sharing, promote participation and benefit for all. These discussions show that global governance should stress co-construction and sharing. On such important occasions as the G20 Summit in Hangzhou, and "The Belt and Road International Cooperation Forum," China has always advocated global governance initiatives such as co-operation, co-construction and sharing.

Xi Jinping says, the basic policy of China's neighbor diplomacy is to keep good relations with its neighbors and keep good company with its neighbors. China will adhere to the principle of "peaceful neighbors, secure neighbors and rich neighbors" and peripheral diplomatic strategy of "amity, sincerity, mutual benefit and inclusiveness." Xi also proposed to promote the establishment of a new international relationship featuring win-win cooperation at the core. Between great powers, there should never be conflict or confrontation, but only mutual respect and win-win cooperation.

All countries, big or small, should treat each other as equals, and practice the code of justice and benefit, and uphold a balanced view of justice and benefit, with justice being more important than benefit.

3. The Historical Parameters of Xi Jinping's Concept of State Governance

(1) Xi Jinping's Thought on State Governance Is a Systematic and Perfect Scientific Theory System.

Xi Jinping's new ideas, new ways of thinking and new strategies constitute a complete system of scientific theories and the latest theoretical result of the development of Marxism in China. It is a theoretical and practical guideline for upholding and developing socialism with Chinese characteristics, for guaranteeing the smooth, continuous advance of all the causes of the Party and the state, as well as for guaranteeing the long-term governance of the party and the long-term stability of the state.

Xi Jinping' s thought on the governance of China is a comprehensive, scientific system of thought. It has creatively formulated solutions to the fundamental, overall and strategic questions confronting the modernization of socialism with Chinese characteristics and the goal of the great rejuvenation of the Chinese nation, basic road, value orientation, development concept, strategic layout, rule of law, the core of leadership, method of reform, national security concept, global governance, etc. Xi's thought on national governance is filled with Marxist ideas and methodology; it is both a world view and view of values, epistemology and methodology. The whole Party, the army and the people of all ethnic groups in the country should equip their minds with such thought, guide their actions, and make new achievements.

In formulating the theory of governance of China, Xi Jinping has made innovations in theory and practice by applying the basic principles of Marxism to the reality of China and the conditions of the present day. Thus, Xi's theory of governance is the latest product of the sinicization of Marxism, a crystallization of the thought and theory based upon a deepened recognition and understanding of the law of communist governance, laws of socialist construction, and laws of development for human society. Xi's theory of national governance has opened up a new realm of the sinicization of Marx doctrine, in that it is a new type of Marxism which may serve as guiding principles for the great struggle in particular historical circumstances. It has accomplished the innovation and development of the theoretical system of socialism with Chinese characteristics, and inherited and sublimated traditional Chinese culture. Therefore, it is a powerful ideological and theoretical weapon to guide all the work of the Party and the state in realizing the great rejuvenation of the Chinese nation. In terms of the historical background, theoretical origin, practical basis, method and mode of thought formation, Xi's theory not only follows the tradition of Marxism-Leninism, Mao Zedong Thought, Deng Xiaoping Theory, the important thought of "Three Represents," and Scientific Development Concept but also advances with the times.

(2) The Epochal Significance of Xi Jinping's Thought on the Governance of China

One important feature of Xi Jinping's thought on the governance of China is the fact that it is solidly based on the reality of contemporary China and the practice of the current times. Xi innovated and developed the theoretical system of socialism with Chinese characteristics by applying the basic principles of Marxist doctrine with theoretical and practical innovation. Therefore, the great epochal significance of Xi's theory of state governance lies in the fact that it is born out of the unique practice of our time and it serves as guiding principles by providing solutions to contemporary issues and problems of the present time.

Right now, China is in a critical stage of realizing the grand "two centenary goals." The first goal of the Chinese dream is to build a moderately prosperous society by the 100th anniversary of the founding of the Chinese Communist Party. The second goal is to build a modernized socialist country by the 100th anniversary of the founding of the People's Republic of China. With these two goals in prospect, the tasks for the country's economic and social development will be arduous indeed. As economic development shifts from high-speed to medium speed, the economy undergoes a structural adjustment and a digestive phase resulting from the early stimulus policies. In addition, the country faces such problems as environmental constraints, construction of moral culture and so on. In the field of Party building and development, over nine decades of development of the Chinese Communist

Party has proved that our Party has always adhered to the essence, ideal, the principles and struggle goals of an authentic Marxist Party, as the Party represents the fundamental interests of the whole nation. It has always dedicated itself to serving the people wholeheartedly, as the Party has always led and united the people in unremitting struggle and great achievement. It is the core of leadership in realizing the cause of socialism with Chinese characteristics. Looking into the future, attention should be paid to such issues as whether our Party is capable of maintaining its youthful vigor, maintaining its progressiveness and purity, and ensuring solidarity and unity of the Party. The above-mentioned national conditions and Party conditions show that the task of reform, development and stability has never been more serious, that we face more contradictions, risks, challenges than before, and that the test of the Party's governance is unprecedented. Xi Jinping's thought on how to run the country has provided theoretical and practical guidance for addressing the above issues and challenges.

Today's world is at the critical stage of global governance, order readjustment, and even reconstruction. In some developed countries, the trend of counter globalization is rising, and the world trade and investment order is facing severe challenges. At the same time, the forces of developing countries are growing, and the global governance system is undergoing profound changes. Confronted with such "chaos" in the global situation, it is no accident that Xi Jinping's concept of "constructing human destiny community" as advocated in his theory of governance has been written into the United Nations resolutions. Currently, China is confronted with a strategic opportunity to lead the world. In this critical and special historical moment, "the Belt and Road Initiative", the notion of constructing human destiny community, the new economic globalization programs and actions proposed and formulated by Xi Jinping will inevitably make tremendous contributions to global governance.

(3) The Far-Reaching Historical Significance of Xi Jinping's Thought on the Governance of China

Xi Jinping's thought on the governance of China has far-reaching historical significance. Only through a broad historical perspective, through logic and vision, can one truly appreciate and grasp its significance. Xi is a Marxist politician with broad historical knowledge and solid cultural training. He is good at deriving the laws from the history of human evolution and apply them to contemporary problems and to the judgment of the trend of future development. Xi Jinping has repeatedly emphasized that "history, reality and the future are interlinked." He said, "China today is developed from yesterday and the day before. To manage China today, we need to have a better understanding of our history and traditional culture. We should positively summarize and explore the ancient wisdom of our country's governance. "With its in-depth exploration of history, firm grasp of the present time and keen vision of the future, and drawing wisdom from all times and from all countries, Xi's thought on governance possesses rich historical significance.

The theoretical formulations of Xi's thought on state governance reflect profound historical insight and clear direction of development. For instance, Xi seeks to explain the reason our Party must uphold and develop socialism with Chinese characteristics in terms of the historical development of socialism in the past five hundred years. He divided the five-hundred-year history of world socialism into six stages, i. e. , the emergence and development of Utopian socialism, the founding of the theoretical system of scientific socialism by Marx and Engels, the victory of the October revolution and the practice of socialism led by Lenin, the gradual formation of the Soviet model, our Party's exploration and practice of socialism after the founding of new China, and the historic decisions our Party has made in pioneering and developing socialism with Chinese characteristics. Xi conceptualizes socialism with Chinese characteristics as one complete stage of the six stages of world socialism, thus clarifying the genesis and destination of socialism with Chinese characteristics. He not only reveals the law of development for socialism with Chinese characteristics, but the tendency of development of world socialism.

Looking back upon the past, we can clearly see that Xi Jinping's theory of state governance epitomizes the experience of five thousand years of Chinese civilization, five hundred years of world socialism, one hundred and seventy years of the struggle for national rejuvenation by the Chinese people, the one hundred years of struggle of the Chinese Communist Party, seventy years' experience of building New China, and forty years of practice in reform and opening up since the Third Plenary Session of the 11th CPC Central Committee. Looking forward to the future, Xi Jinping's thought on the governance of China prophetically answered the questions as to how to realize the "two centenary goals," i.e., the goal of building a moderately prosperous society by 2020 and the goal of modernization by 2049. As to more important strategic issues, Xi has put forward ideas of building a strategic community of human destiny in the international community and pointed out the direction for the realization of the great rejuvenation of the Chinese nation as well as the future direction of human development.

In order to achieve more comprehensive, profound, and thorough research and understanding of Xi Jinping's thought of governing politics, Renmin University of China has organized a group of distinguished scholars and experts to conduct research, discuss, compose, and publish a book series on the "New Concepts, New Ideas and New Strategies of Xi Jinping's Thought on the Governance of China. "Jin Nuo, Party General Secretary of Renmin University, and Liu Wei, President of Renmin University serve as the general editors of the series, with Vice-President Liu Yuanchun and Professor Luo Laijun as designer and organizer to take care of the specific work such as seminars, composition and publication. The authors of the books comprise mostly of research fellows at the Academy of State Development and Strategic Studies, Research Center of the Theoretical System of Socialism with Chinese Characteristics, and Ministry of Education Humanities and Social Sciences Research Base at Renmin University. Divided into ten volumes and with systematic understanding and review of Xi Jinping's thought on national governance as its focus, the book series seeks to present a diverse field of coverage, including theory, economy, politics, rule of law, society, history and culture, science and technology and education, eco-civilization, foreign policy, and Party building, etc. This book series will be published in both Chinese and English, and will be distributed simultaneously at home and abroad, to further promote the study and dissemination of Xi Jinping's thought of governing politics. The series will certainly go a long way toward helping people study and apply Xi Jinping's theory of national governance.

Jin Nuo, Liu Wei
Chief Editors
Beijing, 2017

Introduction

Innovation of Major-Country Diplomacy with Chinese Characteristics

Since the 18th National Congress of the Communist Party of China (CPC), the CPC Central Committee with Comrade Xi Jinping as the core, has accurately grasped the trends of the times and the world, taken into consideration both national and international situations and led the whole nation with strenuous efforts to realize the "Two Centenary Goals"[1] and the Chinese Dream of the great rejuvenation of the Chinese nation. General Secretary Xi Jinping pays high attention to diplomatic work. He has personally introduced the top level design and strategic planning of diplomatic work, and put forward a series of new thoughts, new ideas and new strategies, forming a system of diplomatic thought with distinctive features. Combining historical materialism and dialectical materialism with the reality of China's diplomatic work in the new era and fully absorbing the essence of Chinese traditional culture and the outstanding diplomatic achievements of the New China since 1949, General Secretary Xi Jinping has created a new situation of major-country diplomacy with Chinese characteristics.

Building a community of shared future for mankind is the core and the theoretical basis of Xi Jinping's diplomatic thought, which embodies his grand vision for the progress of the whole world, and by which Xi offers a blueprint for the Chinese solution to the peace and development problems

---

1 The "Two Centenary Goals" are: to finish building a moderately prosperous society in all respects by the time the Communist Party of China celebrates its centenary in 2021; to turn China into a modern socialist country that is prosperous. strong, democratic, culturally advanced, and harmonious by the time the People's Republic of China celebrates its centenary in 2049. Both Goals were advanced at the 18th CPC National Congress. --translator's note

of the present world, expressing China's good wishes and pursuits for an orderly world structure. The concept of a community of shared future for mankind has both distinctive Chinese characteristics and shared values of all mankind. It advocates that every country in the pursuit of their own interests should also take into account the interests of other countries, and form an inseparable bond of shared future, so that they will work together for common development. This concept is of great guiding significance to both contemporary international relations and the development of China.

The establishment of a new model of international relations featuring win-win cooperation is Xi Jinping's blueprint for foreign relations. The new model of international relations and the community of shared future for mankind draw on and enrich each other, and both embody China's aspiration to make our world a better place and its tireless pursuit of this goal. The new model of international relations embodies China's basic proposition for international relations, and expounds China's principled position of diplomacy in the new era.

The community of shared future for mankind is the goal of the new model of international relations, and reflects China's views of the world and of international order from a more macroscopic perspective, which has richer connotations in terms of politics, economy, security, civilization, ecology and many other aspects.

Implementing the values of friendship, justice and shared interests is the value orientation of Xi Jinping's diplomatic thought. This value orientation not only inherits and promotes the brilliant traditional morality and ethical standards of the Chinese culture, but also adds new contents to the treasure house of mankind's shared values. The idea and practice of implementing the values of friendship, justice and shared interests well establishes the moral foundation for exploring a new model of diplomacy with Chinese characteristics. Leading the reform of the global governance system is a major practical innovation in Xi Jinping's diplomatic thought system. It is an important way to construct a new model of international relations featuring win-win cooperation. China's goal of promoting the reform of the global governance system is to prompt the evolution of international order and global governance towards a direction which is more just, rational and conducive to developing countries. At present, as a participant, builder and contributor to the global governance system, China has played a leading role in the process of the reform.

Proposing the Belt and Road Initiative is another strategic innovation in Xi Jinping's diplomatic thought system. It is a systematic project for building both a community of shared future for mankind and a new model of international relations. Combining the Chinese Dream of rejuvenating the Chinese nation and the beautiful dream of peoples in the world to pursue development and prosperity, it is also a comprehensive grand national strategy that integrates domestic development with international cooperation, promotes the interaction between politics and economy, creates the land-sea as well as domestic-foreign linkages and opens the channels between the east and the west, reflecting the remarkable resourcefulness and wisdom of the new generation of Chinese leaders who accurately grasp the profound changes in the world situation and open up a broad space for development.

Xi Jinping's diplomatic thought is an important part of his thought on governing the country as General Secretary of the CPC Central Committee. It not only provides the theoretical basis and the guide to action for the pioneering and enterprising development of China's diplomatic practice, but also stands out as an important innovation in the theory of international relations, which will cast a profound impact on the cause of human development and progress. General Secretary Xi Jinping pointed out, "China should develop a distinctive diplomatic approach befitting its role of a major country. We should, on the basis of summing up our past practice and experience, enrich and further develop principles guiding our diplomatic work, and conduct diplomacy with a salient Chinese feature and a Chinese vision."[2] "Major-country diplomacy" means that China should highlight its role as a major emerging developing country in foreign contacts and be bold in assuming responsibilities. "Chinese feature" means that China should take a different diplomatic path from that of the traditional major countries in history, which highlights such distinctive characteristics of China's diplomacy as valuing peace, development, cooperation and win-win result. These characteristics are imbued with the unique wisdom from Chinese traditional philosophy, history and culture, and make it possible for China to share peace and development with all countries in the world while realizing its own peaceful development and national rejuvenation. Under the leadership of the CPC Central Committee with Comrade Xi Jinping as

---

2 The central conference on work relating to foreign affairs was held in Beijing. People's Daily. 2014-11-30.

the core, China's diplomacy has been more striving, mature and confident since the 18th CPC National Congress[3], accomplishing a series of significant achievements, opening a new chapter in China's diplomacy as a major country with Chinese characteristics and building an all-round, multilevel, and three-dimensional diplomatic layout.

First, China's diplomacy has strengthened the bonds of good neighborliness and friendship. Neighborhood diplomacy occupies a top priority in the overall layout of China's diplomacy because neighborhood areas are a demonstration for the implementation of China's diplomatic concept as a major country with Chinese characteristics. The Belt and Road Initiative raised by General Secretary Xi Jinping in 2013 has received popular response from neighboring countries because it involves above all the all-round cooperation between China and them. On this basis, the Seminar on the Work of Neighborhood Diplomacy was held on October 25, 2013, the first of its kind since the founding of the People's Republic of China in 1949. The Seminar made a comprehensive plan and deployment of the goals, basic principles and train of thought of China's neighborhood diplomacy, putting forward the basic policy to treat them as friends and partners, to make them feel secure and support their development. This policy is characterized by friendship, sincerity, reciprocity and inclusiveness. General Secretary Xi Jinping has left his footprints all over the neighboring countries and regions for expanding China's radiation capacity and influence, and forming a multi-level community of shared future between China and its neighbors.

Second, China's diplomacy has well planned and managed the major-country relations in the chess game of international relations. General Secretary Xi Jinping's concept of building a new model of major-country relations has promoted the strategic mutual trust between China and the United States, enhanced the strategic complementarity between China and Russia, and facilitated the strategic interaction between China and Europe, winning a favorable position for China in a new round of major-country relations adjustment. It has been demonstrated that to achieve long-term stable cooperation, mutual benefit and win-win result, China and the US must respect each other's core interests and major concerns. China-Russia comprehensive strategic partnership has been promoted to an even higher level,

---

3   The 18th CPC National Congress began on November 8. 2012 and closed on November 14. 2012. --translator's note

setting a good example for major countries to deepen their cooperation in the new era. China and the EU have joined hands in developing four major partnerships for peace, growth, reform and civilization between China and the EU, and Sino-British, Sino-French and Sino-German exchanges and cooperation in various fields continue to achieve new results. The New Development Bank (NDB) and Contingency Reserve Arrangement (CRA) have been officially created, and the cooperation between China and such emerging major countries as the BRICS countries has shown a strong momentum.

Third, China's diplomacy has deepened its cooperation with developing countries. Strengthening its solidarity and cooperation with developing countries grows both from the tradition of China's diplomacy and out of the need to jointly safeguard the interests of developing countries. China has achieved full coverage of the all round cooperation mechanism with developing countries, and has built a network of distinctive and focused partnerships with them. Under the guidance of the sound values of friendship, justice and shared interests, China insists on keeping sincere and friendly relationships with developing countries, and on treating each other as equals. China has also been committed to further strengthening high level exchanges, reinforcing dialogue and consultation at different levels, and comprehensively enhancing the friendly and cooperative relations with developing countries. Today, China-Africa relations have reached a stage of growth unmatched in history. China has pursued a foreign policy on Africa featuring sincerity and affinity, given play to the role of the Forum on China-Africa Cooperation (FOCAC), and pushed on the 10 major China-Africa cooperation plans. China and Latin American countries have established the China-Latin America comprehensive cooperative partnership of equality, mutual benefit and common development, and strived to build up a Five-in-One new pattern of China-Latin American relations: sincerely trusting each other in politics, cooperating with each other for a win-win result in economy and trade, learning from each other in people-to-people exchanges, closely cooperating with each other in international affairs, and supporting each other in overall cooperation and bilateral relations. China-Arab relations are at a new starting point that connects the preceding and the following, carries on the past and opens a way for future with peace and cooperation, openness and inclusiveness, learning from each other, mutual benefit and win-win results being the important features in their development. China and the Pacific Islands have established a strategic partnership of mutual respect and common development.

Fourth, China has contributed to the reform of the global governance system. The current global governance system cannot effectively cope with the spread of global problems, providing a strategic opportunity for China to participate in global governance reform and seek global governance leadership. China advocates the concept of "extensive consultation, joint contribution and shared benefits" in global governance and actively promotes the global governance system towards a more just, reasonable and effective direction. In the field of political security and social development, China firmly upholds the authority and status of the UN and supports the central role of the UN in international affairs. In the economic field, China accelerates the reform of the global international economic organizations with the International Monetary Fund (IMF) and the World Trade Organization CWTO) as the cores, and takes positive measures to build the G20 into a stabilizer for world economy, a catalyst for global growth and a driving mechanism for global governance. In the field of inter-national finance, China has initiated the establishment of the Asian Infrastructure Investment Bank (AIIB) and taken part in the establishment of new international financial mechanisms such as the NDB, which provide new thinking for global governance and new solutions to related problems. These are significant contributions made by China to the reform of the global governance system.

Fifth, China has set out to implement the Belt and Road Initiative. The Belt and Road Initiative borrows the historical symbol of the ancient Silk Road and integrates new meanings of the new era into it, creating a new type of international cooperation model, which both guides China's domestic medium and long-term economic and social development, and forges an international community of shared future for mankind. Implementing the Belt and Road Initiative embodies both China's proposition of safeguarding the open world economy to achieve diversity, autonomy, balance and sustainable development, and China's proposition to strengthen cultural exchanges and mutual understanding, and to maintain world peace and stability. The initiative fully deserves to be called a major innovation in China's national strategy in that it is the cohesion of the creative thinking of China's major-country diplomacy with Chinese characteristics.

Since the 18ᵗʰ CPC National Congress, the major-country diplomacy with Chinese characteristics has achieved fruitful results. As a result, a favorable external environment and strategic support for the domestic development has been created, China's sovereignty and security effectively has been safeguarded, and China's international influence significantly has been enhanced. Under the guidance of Xi Jinping's diplomatic thought, the major-country diplomacy with Chinese characteristics will continue to develop forward. "China will continue to be an anchor of international stability, an engine of global growth, a champion of peace and development and a contributor to global governance."[4]

---

4 Quoted from Foreign Minister Wang Yi's answers to questions from domestic and foreign media on China's foreign policy and external relations on 8 March 2017 during the "Two Sessions", namely, the annual sessions of the Chinese People's Political Consultative Conference (CPPCC), which is China's top national advisory body, and the National People's Congress (NPC), the lop legislative body. See Foreign Minister Wang Yi Answered Questions from Domestic and Foreign Media on China's Foreign Policy and External Relations. People's Daily. 2017-03-08.

Chapter 1

Forging the Concept of a Community of Shared Future for Mankind

The idea of building a community of shared future for mankind is the top-level design of Xi Jinping's diplomatic thought, which embodies his grand vision for the progress of the whole world, and by which Xi offers a Chinese blueprint for the solution to the peace and development problems of the present world, expressing China's good wishes and pursuits for an orderly world structure.

1. The proposition and connotations of the idea of "a community of shared future for mankind"

The idea of "a community of shared future" was already used to illustrate China's new perspective on the trends of the world in the white paper of China's Peaceful Development which was published in September, 2011.

It should find new perspectives from the angle of a community of shared future for mankind, sharing weal and woe and pursuing mutually beneficial cooperation, exploring new ways to enhance exchanges and mutual learning among different civilizations, identifying new dimensions in the common interests and values of mankind, and looking for new ways to handle multiple challenges through cooperation among countries and realize inclusive development.[1]

---

1 Information Office of the State Council of the People's Republic of China, China's peaceful development. Beijing: People's Publishing House. 2011: 24.

The report of the 18th CPC National Congress clearly put forward the concept of a community of shared future for mankind, saying that "we should raise awareness of building a community of shared future for mankind. A country should accommodate the legitimate concerns of others when pursuing its own interests, and it should promote common development of all countries when advancing its own development."[2]

Since the 18th CPC National Congress, General Secretary Xi Jinping has constantly explained and improved the concept of a community of shared future for mankind by enriching and developing its theoretical connotations.

On March 23, 2013, President Xi Jinping delivered a speech at Moscow State Institute of International Relations, elaborated for the first time on China's thinking on the future of mankind: "It is a world where countries are linked with and depend on each other at a level never seen before. Human beings, by living in the same global village within the same time and space where history and reality meet, has increasingly emerged as a community of shared future for mankind in which everyone has in himself a little bit of others."[3]

On October 3, 2013, President Xi Jinping addressed Indonesia's parliament, expounding a five-point proposal to build an all-round China-ASEAN community of shared future in the speech entitled "Jointly Build a China-ASEAN Community of Common Destiny".

On the Central Conference on Work Relating to Foreign Affairs held from November 28 to 29, 2014, General Secretary Xi Jinping proposed to turn "China's neighborhood areas into a community of shared future for mankind" in China's external strategic layout.

On March 29, 2015, at the Boao Forum for Asia Annual Conference 2015, President Xi Jinping pointed out in his keynote speech that,

> We have only one planet, and countries share one world. To do well, Asia and the world could not do without each other. Facing the fast changing international and regional landscapes, we must see the whole picture, follow the trend of our times and jointly build a regional order that is more favorable to Asia and the world. We should, through efforts towards such a community for Asia, promote a community of shared future for mankind. In this way, he clarified the relationship between a community of common future for Asia

---

2   HU J T. Firmly march on the path of socialism with Chinese characteristics and strive to complete the building of a moderately prosperous society in all respects: report to the 18th National Congress of the CPC. People's Daily, 2012-11-18 (1).

3   XI J P. The governance of China. Beijing: Foreign Languages Press. 2014: 272.

and a community for mankind.[4]

On April 21, 2015, in his speech at the Parliament of Pakistan entitled "Building a China-Pakistan Community of Shared Destiny to Pursue Closer Win-Win Cooperation", President Xi Jinping stressed that both countries need to work together to substantiate the China-Pakistan community of shared future, so as to lead the way in building a community of shared future in Asia. China-Pakistan relations have become the first group of bilateral relations that have been given the substance of a community of shared future.

On September 28, 2015, addressing the General Debate of the UN General Assembly commemorating the 70th anniversary of the UN in his important speech entitled "Working Together to Forge a New Partnership of Win-Win Cooperation and Create a Community of Shared Future for Mankind", President Xi Jinping linked building a community of shared future for mankind with the establishment of a new type of international relations, and for the first time systematically elaborated the five pillars in constructing a community of shared future for mankind.

On November 30, 2015, when addressing the Paris Conference on Climate Change at the opening ceremony, President Xi Jinping regarded the Paris Agreement as an inspiration to build a community of shared future for mankind, and called on all countries to work together to build it.

On December 16, 2015, in his keynote speech at the opening ceremony of the Second World Internet Conference, President Xi Jinping said, "Cyberspace is the common space of activities for mankind. The future of cyberspace should be in the hands of all countries. Countries should step up for communication, broaden consensus and deepen cooperation to jointly build a community of shared future in cyberspace."[5]

On April 2, 2016, President Xi Jinping pointed out at the Fourth Nuclear Security Summit in Washington D. C. that, "Under the precondition of respect for national sovereignty, all countries should participate in nuclear security affairs, and adopt an open and inclusive spirit to forge a community of shared future on nuclear security.[6]

---

4   XI J P. Towards a community of shared future and a new future for Asia. People's Daily, 2015-03-29 (2).

5   XI J P. Remarks at the Opening Ceremony of the Second World Internet Conference. People's Daily, 2015-12-17 (2).

6   XI J P. Strengthen global nuclear security architecture and promote global nuclear security governance: speech given at the Nuclear Security Summit in Washington DC. People's Daily. 2016-04-03(2).

On January 18, 2017, President Xi Jinping delivered a speech of "Working Together to Build a Community of Shared Future for Mankind" at the UN Headquarters in Geneva, in which he pointed out,

> Pass on the torch of peace from generation to generation, sustain development and make civilization flourish: this is what people of all countries longed for; it is also the responsibility statesmen of our generation ought to shoulder. And China's proposition is: build a community of shared future for mankind and achieve shared and win-win development.[7]

With General Secretary Xi Jinping's repeated in-depth explanation, from a community of shared future between countries, to a community of shared future within a region, then to a community of shared future for mankind, the levels and connotations of the concept have been enriched, interrelated and interdependent, each with a particular focus, covering multiple fields such as politics, security, development, civilization, ecology and cyberspace. China forges a community of shared future not only with many neighboring countries and developing countries, but also with other developed countries such as the New Zealand, France and Germany. In addition to advocating the Asian community of shared future, China has also raised such ideas as the China-ASEAN Community of Shared Future, the China-Arab Community of Shared Future, the China-African Community of Shared Future, and the China-Latin American Community of Shared Future.

We only have one earth, and it is the only home for all countries. There are still many contradictions and conflicts in the world today, but peace, development, cooperation and win-win result are world trends. Never before has China been so close to the center of the world stage as it is today, and never before has it been so closely connected with the future of the outside world as it is today. Building a community of shared future for mankind is a lofty cause that focuses on the progress of all mankind, and aims at both China's long-term development and the world's prosperity and stability. In short, a community of shared future for mankind refers to the formation of an interdependent and interlinked state in which every country in the world should take into account the interests of other countries in the pursuit of its own interests, seek common development and cooperation, enhance the common interests of all mankind, and jointly promote progress of all

---

7   XI J P. Work together to build a community of shared future for mankind: speech given at the United Nations Headquarters in Geneva. People's Daily. 2017-01-20(2).

mankind. Specifically, a community of shared future for mankind refers to the association of all countries in the world characterized by such features as interdependence, equality, win-win result and inclusiveness.

The first feature is interdependence. "In today's world, interaction and interdependence is the general trend. With cross-border flows of goods, capital, information and people, regardless of distance, size and level of development, countries are increasingly finding themselves in a community of common interests and shared future, based on intertwined interests and common challenges."[8] all countries have formed a bond of interests due to interdependence, and they all rise and fall together. No country can pursue its own interests and ignore the interests of other countries and the public interests of the world.

The second feature 's equality. A community of shared future for mankind means that all countries treat and respect each other as equals.

> Countries may differ in size, strength or level of development, but they are all equal members of the international community with equal rights to participate in regional and international affairs. On matters that involve us all, we should discuss and look for a solution together. Being a big country means shouldering greater responsibilities for regional and world peace and development, as opposed to seeking greater monopoly over regional and world affairs.[9]

The third feature is win-win result. "A country which pursues its own development, security and well-being must also let other countries pursue their development, security and well-being."[10] In the face of financial crises, terrorism, natural disasters, climate change and other global issues, it is hardly possible for any country to manage alone; all countries in the world need to pull together. The right way is that major countries support minor countries, and rich countries aid poor countries. By helping each other out all countries can achieve common development.

---

8   XI J P. Work together to promote openness, inclusiveness and peaceful development: speech given at dinner hosted by the lord mayor of the city of London. People's Daily. 2015-10-23 (2).
9   XI J P. Towards a community of common destiny and a new future for Asia: keynote speech given at the Boao Forum for Asia Annual Conference 2015. People's Daily. 2015-03-28 (2).
10   XI J P. Work together to maintain world peace and security: speech given at the opening ceremony of the World Peace Forum. People's Daily. 2012-07-08 (2).

The fourth feature is inclusiveness. The world is rich and colorful. And all countries should fully respect the diversity of different nationalities, religions and civilizations, and fully respect the social system and development path of one another's independent choice."Each civilization represents the unique vision and contribution of its people, and no civilization is superior to others. Different civilizations should have dialogues and exchanges instead of trying to exclude or replace each other."[11] The world is big enough to accommodate the common development and sharing of security of all countries in the world.

2. The origin of the concept of a community of shared future for mankind

As a new concept of the international order, the idea of a community of shared future for mankind has a profound ideological basis. It is rooted in China's long history and culture, drawing on the connotations of socialist theory with Chinese characteristics, and assimilating and sublimating the essence of China's outstanding diplomatic traditions.

First, the idea of a community of shared future for mankind inherits the preponderant "Under-Heaven" (天下　tianxia) feeling that has been cultivated in the Chinese thought for thousands of years, and contains the traditional Chinese political philosophy of "living in harmony with other nations" (協和萬邦　xiehe wanbang) and "great harmony under heaven" (天下大同　tianxia datong). Stretching for thousands of years, China's history has given birth to a unique culture, embodying rich political philosophy as well as philosophy of life, endowing the Chinese nation with strong vitality. The ideal that "when the great way prevails, all things under heaven are shared equally and justly" communicates the Chinese sense of responsibility that goes beyond national boundaries. The idea of "never imposing on others what you do not desire" states the Chinese principle of mutual respect and non-interference. The creed of "practicing self-cultivation, bringing the family to unison, governing the state and establishing peace under heaven" stresses Chinese use of the power of inherent moral cultivation, civilization and education to achieve the goal of world peace. The propositions of "seeking harmony but not uniformity" and "endeavoring in concert when confronted with difficulties" reveal Chinese people's value orientations of

11   XI J P. Speeches at the Series of Summits Marking the 70th Anniversary of the United Nations. Beijing: People's Publishing House. 2015: 18.

openness and inclusiveness, harmonious coexistence, and seeking common ground while reserving differences. The determination to "be the first to worry about the troubles under heaven" shows Chinese people's aspirations to do good to mankind. The pursuit that "while in success, try to benefit others" carries the responsible sense of sharing. The lofty sentiment that "all the people of the world are brothers" expresses Chinese people's simple wish for equality. The unique culture with a history of thousands of years has created the spiritual pursuit of the Chinese nation and built a spiritual home for the Chinese. It plays an important role in educating and encouraging the Chinese people and in concentrating the nation in the long history. "At the same time, the rich philosophical thought, the humanistic spirit, the civilizing thought and the moral ideas in the Chinese traditional culture are also imbued with important clues to solve the problems faced by the contemporary people. It can provide beneficial hints for people to understand and transform the world, bring useful inspiration on how to govern the country, and give useful suggestions on how to enhance our moral construction."[12] By carrying forward the essence of Chinese traditional culture and exploring the convergence point of traditional Chinese culture and the contemporary era, we can pool Chinese wisdom to help the international community deal with various problems and challenges. The cultural core of a community of shared future for mankind is the brilliant Chinese traditional culture, which is featured by moderation and peacefulness. "The pursuit of peace, amity and harmony is an integral part of the Chinese character which runs deep in the blood of the Chinese people."[13] The peace-loving thought has shaped the Chinese national character of non-bullying the weak and upholding sincerity and peace, which have been the basic Chinese beliefs on governing the country since ancient times, and which enjoy strong vitality today and are still China's fundamental philosophy in handling international relations. The world is facing not only the dilemma of material development, but also the deep spiritual crisis of modern civilization. China's unique traditional culture provides a source of continuous spiritual wealth for creating a new concept of international order, and lays a historical and cultural foundation for the idea of a community of shared future for mankind.

---

12 The Publicity Department of the CPC Central Committee. General Secretary Xi Jinping's important remarks (2016 Edition). Beijing: Xuexi Publishing House. 2016: 202.
13 XI J P. Speech at the Körber Foundation, Germany. People's Daily. 2014-03-30 (2).

Second, the theory of socialism with Chinese characteristics acts as a strong ideological guide for the development of the concept of a community of shared future for mankind. "Socialism with Chinese characteristics is the integration of the theory of scientific socialism and social development theories of Chinese history."[14] The theory of socialism with Chinese characteristics not only guides the practice of socialist modernization in contemporary China, but also inspires the theoretical thinking and innovation in accordance with the change of the times and the problems in practice. The relationship between China and the world is a major issue related to the success or failure of the socialist cause.

> Today's world is witnessing profound and complex changes and China is in unprecedentedly close contact and interaction with the world. In this context, we should pay close attention to the changes of the international situation, grasp the overall domestic and international situations, take the initiative in the trend of the times and achieve development.[15]

The concept of a community of shared future for mankind is the product of General Secretary Xi Jinping's deep thinking on the relationship between China and the world and on the process of human civilization, which necessarily reflects the essential attributes of the theory of socialism with Chinese characteristics.

"The characteristics of China's diplomacy are rooted in the socialist ideas that China upholds."[16] The Marxist view of social history holds that human beings will eventually unite themselves and by this unity achieve solidarity and friendship between and common prosperity of all nations. From the perspective of the pursuit of an ideal human society, the concept of a community of shared future for mankind is a type of internationalism with distinctive socialist characteristics. Unlike the unequal center-margin structure of the international economic relations used to be dominated by Western countries, nor the liberalist solution which aggressively pushes Western values in the name of universal values, the concept of a community of shared future for mankind promotes sovereign equality and all-inclusiveness,

---

14   XI J P. The governance of China. Beijing: Foreign Languages Press. 2014: 21.
15   The Publicity Department of the CPC Central Committee. General Secretary Xi Jinping's Important Remarks (2016 Edition). Beijing: Xuexi Publishing House. 2016: 39.
16   WANG Y. Exploring the path of major-country diplomacy with Chinese characteristics. International studies. 2013: 4.

emphasizing respect for diversity, advocating the establishment of parallel partnership between countries, and sharing both opportunities for development and the risk costs. It proposes that different development models should learn from each other in mutual emulation, reflecting the positive significance of the path of socialism with Chinese characteristics to the world's development.

Third, the idea of a community of shared future for mankind is an innovation of the New China's outstanding diplomatic thoughts. Since the founding of the New China in 1949, its diplomacy has covered an extraordinary course of more than sixty years. Whatever the changes happened in the international situation, the New China's diplomacy has always adhered to the independent foreign policy of peace, and has gradually formed a series of Chinese world views and basic concepts of international relations in its diplomatic practice, including the Five Principles of Peaceful Coexistence, seeking common ground while reserving differences, the "three worlds" strategic thinking, not seeking hegemony, non-alignment, practicing democracy in international relations, the path of peaceful development, and harmonious world, to name a few. These brilliant diplomatic thoughts and ideas are the driving force and guide for China's diplomacy to move forward.

China is the first country in the world to have advocated a new type of international order. The Five Principles of Peaceful Coexistence were first proposed by China in the 1950s and co-sponsored with India and Myanmar, which impacted the old world order characterized by great powers seeking hegemony during the Cold War. When China's modernization drive had just started, Mao Zedong pointed out that "China should have a greater contribution to mankind"[17], fully demonstrating China's lofty value orientation, responsibility and commitment. After the reform and opening-up, Deng Xiaoping, on the basis of comprehensively analyzing various contradictions and interrelations of international relations, put forward the scientific conclusion that peace and development are the two major strategic issues in today's world, therefore increasingly linking the future of China closely with that of the world through opening up to the outside world. After the end of the Cold War, China made it clear that a more just and reasonable new international order based on the Five Principles of Peaceful Coexistence should be established, that each country's domestic

---

17　MAO Z D. In Commemoration of Mr. Sun Yat-sen. People's Daily. 2005-09-16 (1).

affairs should be decided by its people themselves, that the world's affairs should be negotiated on an equal footing by all countries, and that global challenges should be dealt with cooperatively by all countries. In the 21st century, China further proposed that "we should endeavor to preserve the diversity of civilizations in the spirit of equality and openness, make international relations more democratic and jointly build towards a harmonious world where all civilizations coexist and accommodate with each other"[18] The concept of a community of shared future for mankind is the inheritance and development of the concept of peaceful diplomacy that China has always maintained, reflecting the ethical pursuit and the sense of responsibility for the future of the world that have been constant in China's diplomacy. It is the responsibility of China's diplomacy to uphold fairness, defend justice and promote righteousness. It is the mission of China's diplomacy to maintain peace and development of the world and to promote the international order in a more fair and reasonable direction. It is the vision of China's diplomacy to take the common interests of mankind as the starting point and reflect on the prospect and future of the world.

3. The realistic foundation of building a community of shared future for mankind

The current general trends of international relations lay a solid practical foundation for building a community of shared future for mankind. Since the beginning of the 21st century, international relations have witnessed both coexistence and contests between such complex situations as unipolarity and multi polarity, confrontation and dialogue, conflict and cooperation, and turmoil and stability. However, in the light of long-term development, only those with global importance can determine the trends and directions of world development. In the face of world multi polarization, in-depth development of economic globalization, cultural diversity and the advance of social informatization, today's human beings are better equipped than ever before to march toward the goals of peace and development. And forging a community of shared future for mankind is one of the Chinese programs to achieve such goals.

---

18   Hu Jintao Build towards a harmonious world of lasting peace and common prosperity. People's Daily. 2005-09-16 (1).

The multipolarization of the world is a development process of international relations in which the balance of power between the major powers gradually tends to reach a relative balance. This trend is in line with the objective law of unbalanced development of the world. The rise and fall of the world's great powers throughout history demonstrates that there is no fixed pattern in the competition of national strength, nor is there a permanent winner. After the end of the Cold War, the United States became the only superpower with obvious advantages in strength in politics, economy, military, science and information technology. Its hegemonic policy and unilateral actions in international affairs were strengthened, which severely obstructed the world's multi polarization process in the short term. The 2003 Iraq War was the consequence of a vicious expansion of the US unilateralism. However, the evolution of international forces after the end of the Cold War did not result in a unipolar pattern dominated by the United States. In the long run, the US advantage is not absolute. Various forces across the world are constantly evolving, especially the developing countries, whose overall strength has risen markedly, casting greater influences of varying degrees on international affairs. The unilateralist policy runs counter to the trend of today's world and is opposed and resisted by more and more countries and peoples around the world. The future world will not be dominated by a certain country or group of countries, but will be a world in which all countries both compete with one another and cooperate and coexist interdependently, developing side by side. The development of the trend towards multipolarization is a kind of historical progress, in which the hegemony and power politics of a few countries will be constrained, and the developing countries will gain greater say in international affairs, thus promoting the democratization of international relations, safeguarding the world's equal exchanges and cooperation, and creating the conditions for the construction of a community of shared future for mankind.

Economic globalization has been an important feature of the world economy smce the 1990s, which means that the economic resources and production factors of all countries in the world can be effectively arranged on a global scale, and that the integration of such fields as trade, finance, production and even the economic policies of various countries can be deepened by way of complementing each other with their own economic advantages so as to achieve strong growth and prosperity in the world economy. In the context of economic globalization, interdependence between countries and the degree of their mutual dependence have been strengthened, and international cooperation and coordination have become the main theme of the international community. Some of the traditional concepts in the field of international relations have been impacted. Zero-sum thinking is replaced by a win-win model and the "either-or" rules of international contacts give way to the new idea that countries stand and fall together. In the context of economic globalization, economic crises are so conductive that one country's crisis may quickly lead to a chain reaction, spread to other countries, and even endanger the world economy. In this context, no country can place itself out of the international community, or be divorced from the world market; any country's economic development and even survival is more or less dependent on other countries. Coordination and cooperation have become the major means of dealing with inter-state contradictions and conflicts, and are an important guarantee for the promotion of peace and the prevention of conflict. The world has become a "global village" in its true sense. All countries in the world share one another's weal or woe in terms of interests, their internal and external affairs more open and transparent to one another and global awareness widely disseminated. In short, "in the era of economic globalization, there is no island completely cut off from the rest of the world. As members of the global village, we need to cultivate the awareness of a community of shared future for mankind."[19] Economic globalization provides a practical possibility to create a community of shared future for mankind.

Cultural diversity refers to the richness of human culture in its manifestations. According to the Universal Declaration on Cultural Diversity adopted by the General Conference of the UNESCO at its 31st Session in 2001, cultural diversity is a common heritage of humanity and should be recognized and affirmed for the benefit of present and future generations. The countries all over the world have created a variety of colorful culture in the long history of their development. They have differences in social system, values, degree of development, historical tradition, religious belief and cultural background. Each country and nation has its own characteristics and strengths. Each country and nation should cherish and maintain its

---

19   XI J P. A new starting point for China's development a new blueprint for global growth: keynote speech given at the opening ceremony of the B 20 Summit. People's Daily. 2016-09-01 (3).

own ideology and culture as well as recognize and respect the ideologies and cultures of other countries and nations. The ideology and culture of every country and nation, regardless of its strength or size, should be recognized and respected. Respect for diversity is the prerequisite for the democratization of international relations.

> As to the various civilizations created by the human society, we should adopt a learning attitude and actively absorb the beneficial components, co-ordinating all fine cultural genes created by mankind and modern culture, using them to adapt to modern society, and carrying forward the outstanding cultural spirits that span time and space, go beyond the country, are full of eternal charm and conform to contemporary values.[20]

Diversification is the driving force and source of the world's development. History has repeatedly proved that no attempt to solve cultural diversity by coercive means can succeed, and such attempts only bring disasters to the world. Only by forging a community of shared future for mankind, respecting cultural diversity, learning from each other, seeking common ground while reserving differences, living in harmony and promoting each other, can human beings create a colorful and prosperous world.

Social informatization refers to the process of fully achieving informatization in all fields of the human society in the information age, in which information resources are exploited and utilized maximally, the level of information technology application in the fields of social life is improved, and higher quality products and service arc provided for the society. According to the history of social development, mankind had experienced the agricultural revolution and the industrial revolution, and is now facing up with the information revolution. The agricultural revolution strengthened human beings' viability, making them advance from foraging and hunting to farming and domesticating, from barbarianism to civilization. The industrial revolution expanded human beings' physical strength, replaces their physical labor with machinery and the manual production of individual workshops with large-scale factory production. And the information revolution enhanced the human brain, bringing another qualitative leap of productivity, making profound impact on the development in such areas as international politics,

---

20　XI J P. Address to the international conference commemorating the 2565th Anniversary of Confucius and the 18th Congress of the International Confucian Association. People's Daily. 2014-09-25 (2).

economy, culture, society, ecology and military affairs. As General Secretary Xi Jinping pointed out,

> Amid a new round of scientific and technological revolution with information technology at its core, the Internet is increasingly becoming a pacesetter of innovation-driven development, profoundly changing people's way of production and life and powering social development. It has turned the world into a global village and made the international community a highly interdependent community of common destiny.[21]

The progress of human society depends to a certain extent on the ability of human beings to understand and use resources. Information being a new resource, the development and application of the information technology is regarded to be endless. Informatization of the society closely connects all mankind, and internet connection and information exchange have laid a good technological foundation for a community of shared future for mankind.

These developments are intertwined, greatly improving social productivity, promoting the democratization of international relations, and becoming the driving force for the international community to move towards a community of shared future for mankind. At the same time, the global problems that threaten the survival and development of all mankind have become increasingly prominent. Environmental pollution, climate change, food security, population explosion, drug abuse, income disparity, international terrorism and other issues are becoming increasingly serious. Internet security, outer space exploration, polar development and other new problems are even more challenging. Global issues are too universal, holistic, complicated and highly interconnected for a single country to deal with alone. Nor is it possible for any country to keep out of the way. All countries around the world need to join hands and work together in a responsible spirit to meet these challenges. However, the current international system under the auspices of the Western countries cannot effectively deal with the spreading global problems. The so-called "universal value" concept by the Western countries cannot meet the practical needs of diversified development in the 21st century. China, for the common interests of all mankind, conforms to

---

21 Jointly foster a peaceful, secure, open and cooperative cyberspace and build a multilateral, democratic and transparent global internet governance system. People's Daily. 2014-11-20 (1).

the development trend of the world, advocates and disseminates the idea of building a community of shared future for mankind to the international community, by which it actively responds to the serious challenges of global problems and fulfills its international obligations as a responsible major country.

4. Establishing the path to a community of shared future for mankind

In September 2015, at the Series of Summits Marking the 70th Anniversary of the United Nations, President Xi Jinping elaborated on the path of building a community of shared future for mankind from five aspects: building partnerships in which countries treat each other as equals, engage in mutual consultation and show mutual understanding; creating a security architecture featuring fairness, justice, joint contribution and shared benefits; promoting open, innovative and inclusive development that benefits all; increasing inter-civilization exchanges to promote harmony, inclusiveness and respect for differences; building an ecosystem that puts mother nature and green development first. In January 2017, President Xi Jinping delivered a speech at the United Nations Office in Geneva entitled "Work Together to Build a Community of Shared Future for Mankind", again stressed that, "actions hold the key to building a community of shared future for mankind. To achieve this goal, the international community should promote partnership, security, growth, inter-civilization exchanges and the building of a sound ecosystem."[22]

First of all, the construction of partnerships of dialogue with no confrontation and of friendship rather than alliance is the major path to a community of shared future for mankind. The partnership strategy has been an important part of China's diplomacy after the end of the Cold War. It follows the basic principles of mutual respect and seeking common ground while reserving differences and the association principle of reaching consensus through communication and negotiation, and pursues harmonious relations featured by mutual assistance and cooperation, mutual benefit and common development between partners. Different from the exclusive alliance, partnership is a new model of bilateral relations of cooperation. It does

---

22 XI J P. Work together to build a community of shared future for mankind: speech given at the United Nations Headquarter in Geneva. People's Daily. 2017-01-20 (2).

not indicate confrontation or conflict, nor is it directed against an imaginary enemy or a third party. Partnership does not mean that there is no disagreement or contradiction between the two sides, but means that they adhere to communication and treat each other sincerely with their political mutual trust and economic mutual benefit as strategic fulcrums, constantly expand the framework of their common interests, and create conditions for the construction of a community of shared future for mankind through stabilizing their bilateral relations. China devotes itself to "making more friends while abiding by the principle of non-alignment and building a global network of partnerships."[23] Great achievements have been accomplished so far. By the end of 2016, China has established different forms of partnership with 97 countries and international organizations. Despite the differences in formulation and the distinction of content in breadth and the depth of their cooperation, their relationships, such as comprehensive strategic partnerships, strategic partnerships, comprehensive friendly cooperative partnerships, all-round cooperative partnerships and friendly partnerships, are all based on the principles of equality and mutual benefit and non-alignment. With the initially formed network of partnerships, the consensuses at the bilateral level between China and the partner countries can have impacts in a broader framework of multilateral relations which will jointly promote the construction of a community of shared future for mankind.

Second, the achievement of common security is an important guarantee of forging a community of shared future for mankind. In the era of economic globalization, each country's national security is interrelated and affects one another. Security is universal: a country cannot have security while others are in turmoil, nor can some countries have security while other countries are in turmoil. No country can sacrifice the security of other countries to seek the so-called "ab solute security" of its own. It is impossible to create a community of shared future for mankind without the security of the international community. President Xi Jinping said: "we should abandon Cold War mentality in all its manifestation and foster a new vision of common, comprehensive, cooperative and sustainable security."[24] Common security means that the safety of every country is respected and protected.

---

23   The central conference on work relating to foreign affairs was held in Beijing. People's Daily. 2014-11-30 (1).
24   Speeches by Xi Jinping at the Series of Summits Marking the 70th Anniversary of the United Nations. Beijing: People's Publishing House. 2015: 16-17.

Comprehensive security means that the security of both traditional fields and non-traditional fields is coordinated and maintained. Cooperative security means that disputes are settled in a peaceful way, and strategic mutual trust is enhanced through dialogue and cooperation, seeking peace and promoting safety through cooperation. Sustainable security means that importance is attached to both development and safety issues so as to achieve lasting security, development being the foundation of security, and security the precondition for development."The tree of peace does not grow on barren land, and the ruins of development are not harvested amidst the flames of war."[25] This new vision of security aims to create a fair, just and shared security framework, and promote the realization of a community of shared future for mankind.

Third, adherence to common development is the cornerstone of building a community of shared future for mankind. Development is the core issue of the world today. The gap between the rich and the poor and the issue of poverty caused by the unbalanced development of the world economy hinder the overall prosperity of the world economy and arc not conducive to the maintenance of world peace and stability or the building of common security. Meanwhile, the connotations of the development concept have been continuously expanded. From the simple pursuit of rapid economic growth to the implementation of the simultaneous development of both society and economy, and to the emphasis on the coordinated development of economy, society and environment, the concept of sustainable development dominates the current agenda of global development. Therefore, President Xi Jinping proposed: "development is meaningful only when it is inclusive and sustainable. To achieve such development requires openness, mutual assistance and win-win coop."[26] China has always advocated that, in international economic cooperation, confrontation should be replaced by cooperation , and monopoly should be substituted by the win-win result. China has been striving to integrate the needs of its own economic construction with the interests of other countries' economic development , sharing the interests of development with other countries , adhering to the common development of all countries and seeking the prospect of an open and innovative, inclusive and reciprocal world economy. Confronted with such issues as imbal-

25 XI J P. The governance of China. Beijing: Foreign Languages Press. 2014: 356.
26 Speeches by Xi Jinping at the Series of Summits Marking the 70th Anniversary of the United Nations. Beijing: People's Publishing House, 2015: 17.

anced development, unfairness and injustice brought about by economic globalization, China advocates an open, inclusive, reciprocal, balanced and win-win model of economic globalization, promoting all countries from communities of closely linked interests to a community of shared future with common concerns.

Fourth, enhancement of exchanges and mutual learning between civilizations is the strong glue that will bind the community of shared future for mankind. There are more than 200 countries and regions, more than 2,500 ethnic groups , and a variety of religions in the world. Different histories, national conditions, nationalities and customs give birth to different civilizations. Each civilization has its unique charm and rich cultural legacy, each is part of mankind's intellectual wealth. A single flower does not make a spring; all flowers blooming together bring the spring to the garden. Civilizations are not differentiated in status or in quality but are only different in their characteristics or geographical locations. "Civilizations have become richer and more colorful with exchanges and mutual learning. Such exchanges and mutual learning form an important drive for human progress and global peace and development."[27] Interactions between civilizations require the spirit of "harmony without uniformity". Only by acknowledging diversity, mutual respect and harmonious coexistence can the world be rich, colorful, prosperous and thriving. Adhering to the equal dialogue between different civilizations and replacing confrontations and conflicts between civilizations with exchanges between civilizations , are not only conducive to the transformation of the diversity of and differences between civilizations into a dynamic that accelerates the common development of all countries , but also help push all countries in the world move together towards the goals of peace and development. Mutual learning between different civilizations is a step that goes further than the basis of equal dialogue. No civilization in the world is developed in a completely closed environment, the process of emergence and development of one civilization is at the same time a history of collisions , exchanges and integration with other civilizations. Only by drawing from other civilizations and absorbing the essence of other civilizations can we really build a community of shared future for mankind in which all civilizations flourished.

---

27   XI J P. The governance of China. Beijing: Foreign Languages Press. 2014: 258.

Fifth, promotion of ecology is a prerequisite for the creation of a community of shared future for mankind. The ecological environment is the external space and material foundation for the survival and development of human beings. The progress of industrial civilization and the high degree of development of science and technology have brought a lot of serious environmental problems while creating unprecedented varieties of material wealth for mankind. The earth is an integral ecosystem , and the environmental problem is not only endangering a single country or region , but also threatening the survival and development of all mankind and putting their common interests at risk. "To build a sound ecology is vital for mankind ' s future. All members of the international community should work together to build a sound global eco-environment. We should respect nature, follow nature's ways and protect nature. We should firmly pursue green, low-carbon, circular and sustainable development."[28] Only in this way can all countries solve the contradictions brought about by industrial civilization and realize the new pattern of harmony between the man and the nature. The ecological environment is a productive force, too. To protect and improve the eco-environment is to protect and develop the productive force. At the Fifth Plenary Session of the 18th CPC Central Committee, General Secretary Xi Jinping put forward five ideas of development, including innovation, coordination, green, openness and sharing. As a basic concept of China's economic and social development, the idea of green development promotes the country's ecological construction to the height of national development strategy, reflecting China's determination, as well as contribution, to create a community of shared future for mankind.

The process of building a community of shared future for mankind will be long and tortuous. At present, many of the historical and contemporary contradictions in international relations are still deep-rooted and intricate. Hegemonism and power politics still exist, and zero-sum thinking and the Cold War mentality remain stubborn. Cooperation and struggle between countries exist side by side; opposition and confrontation are not uncommon. Although the goal of building a community of shared future for mankind is far from being achieved, the vision "is a forward-looking idea regarding the trend of development in the world. It represents a common aspiration and

---

28   XI J P. Speech at the Series of Summits Marking the 70th Anniversary of the United Nations. Beijing: People's Publishing House. 2015: 18.

common goal of human development and requires long-term efforts of all countries in the world. At the same time, it represents the common value , code of conduct and pathway that countries need to embrace to jointly tackle the current development and security challenges and properly handle state-to-state relations."[29] As a visionary strategic thought, the construction of a community of shared future for mankind has a long way to go. It can only advance step by step in a pragmatical way.

5. The significance of forging a community of shared future for mankind in the contemporary world

The idea of a community of shared future for mankind grows from a strategic judgment made by China based on both its own development needs and world trends. It is in line with the common aspiration and interests of the Chinese people and the peoples across the world. It bears distinctive Chinese characteristics and common values of all mankind, and has an important guiding significance on modern day international relations and the development of China.

First, the vision of building a community of shared future form a kind pointed out the direction for the development and progress of human society. At the commemoration of the 95th anniversary of the founding of the CPC, General Secretary Xi Jinping made it quite clear: "the CPC and Chinese people pledged long ago to make a new and bigger contribution to the human development. Having experienced bitterness in the past, the CPC and the Chinese people know the value of peace and development , and see it as our sacred duty to promote the peaceful development of the world."[30] At present, the world is experiencing a historic transformation. The international order and the global governance system are undergoing profound and complex changes. The framework of a community of shared future for mankind put forward by China addressed the problem of the changing international order and system. What it points to is a bright future where all arc free from want, all have access to development and possess dignity, and all live in a beautiful world of harmony and mutual respect.

<hr>

29 WANG Y. Work together to create a community of shared future for mankind. People's Daily. 2016-03-31 (7).

30 XI J P. Speech at a ceremony marking the 95th Anniversary of the Founding of the Communist Party of China. People's Daily. 2010-07-02 (2).

In 2015, President Xi Jinping stated at the UN General Assembly: "peace, development, equity, justice, democracy and freedom are common values of all mankind."[31] These common values are the goals of mankind's long-term pursuits, and also the value base for the construction of a community of shared future for mankind. China's proposition is a transcendence and innovation of the traditional theory of international relations, which will have a profound impact on the future development of international relations and is of great significance to the progress of human society, world peace and prosperity.

Second, the concept of forging a community of shared future for mankind provides a driving force for the Chinese Dream of the great rejuvenation of the Chinese nation. On November 29, 2012, General Secretary Xi Jinping specified the important idea of "China Dream" when he viewed "The Road toward Renewal" exhibition. "Achieving the rejuvenation of the Chinese nation has been the greatest dream of the Chinese people since the modern times. This dream embodies the long-cherished expectation of several generations of the Chinese people, gives expression to the overall interests of the Chinese nation and the Chinese people, and represents the shared aspiration of all the sons and daughters of the Chinese nation."[32] He emphasized that, "we are now closer to the goal of achieving the rejuvenation of the Chinese nation, and we are more confident and capable of achieving it than at any other time in history."[33] On March 17, 2013, at the First Session of the 12th National People's Congress, General Secretary Xi Jinping summarized the essence and connotations of the Chinese Dream as a threefold goal of "making China prosperous and strong, rejuvenating the nation, and bringing happiness to the Chinese people."[34] As a clear judgment on the strategic goal and development path of the great rejuvenation of the Chinese nation, the Chinese Dream has become the core concept of China's national development strategy. The concept of building a community of shared future for mankind integrates the interests of the Chinese people with the common interests of peoples all over the world and is highly consistent with the purpose and the goal of realizing the great

31   XI J P. Speech at the Series of Summits Marking the 70th Anniversary of the United Nations. Beijing: People's Publishing House. 2015:15.
32   XI J P. The governance of China. Beijing: Foreign Languages Press. 2014: 36 .
33   Ibid. 35-36.
34   XI J P. The governance of China. Beijing: Foreign Languages Press. 2014: 39 .

rejuvenation of the Chinese nation. General Secretary Xi Jinping stressed multiple times that, "the Chinese Dream is a desire for happiness and similar to the dreams of the people of other countries. The people can attain happiness only when their country and nation constantly thrive. China will thrive only when the world prospers."[35] The construction of a community of shared future for mankind endows the Chinese Dream with more profound world significance. This integration of the Chinese Dream with the world dream embodies China's global vision, open mind and sense of responsibility as a major country, which make China consciously unite its own development with the common development of the world.

Third, the idea of building a community of shared future for mankind lays the theoretical foundation for the preliminarily establishment of the theoretical system of major-country diplomacy with Chinese characteristics. Since the 18th National Congress of the CPC , the Central Committee with Comrade Xi Jinping as the core , taking into consideration both the domestic and the international situations, has vigorously promoted innovation in diplomatic theory and practice, stressed that China's external work should have distinctive Chinese characteristics and a Chinese style, and expounded comprehensively and thoroughly on the objectives, principles and path ways of China's diplomacy in the new situation, initially establishing the basic framework of major-country diplomacy with Chinese characteristics. The idea of building a community of shared future for mankind is a core achievement in the theoretical innovation of diplomacy by General Secretary Xi Jinping. It is the product of profound thinking and judgment on the process of human civilization and the prospect of human development. It follows the basic principles of China's diplomatic policies, links China's own prosperity with the world's peaceful development , occupies the high grounds of the development of the times and human morality, comprehensively enhances the goal of China's diplomatic thinking and becomes a banner guiding the major-country diplomacy with Chinese characteristics. Under the guidance of the idea of building a community of shared future for mankind, a succession of major innovations of diplomatic theory have proposed, such as building a new type of international relations with win-win cooperation as the core, practicing the values of friendship, justice and shared interests, promoting the reform of the global governance system,

---

35   Ibid. 64.

and implementing the Belt and Road Initiative, to name a few. These innovations have pushed the development of China's diplomatic theory up to a new historical level, adding to General Secretary Xi Jinping's thought on the China's governance.

Fourth, the idea of building a community of shared future for mankind prepares a guide to action for comprehensively enhancing the practice of major-country diplomacy with Chinese characteristics. In the face of complex and ever-changing international situations with new opportunities and challenges, China's major-country diplomacy with Chinese characteristics aims at the great rejuvenation of the Chinese nation and the construction of a community of shared future for mankind, forges ahead and has built a comprehensive, multi-level and three-dimensional diplomatic layout, creating a new phase in China's diplomatic work. Specific instances are as follows: constructing a community of shared future with neighborhood countries and placing the consolidation of good-neighborly friendship framework in the first position in the overall situation of foreign affairs; advocating a new model of major-country relations and creating a healthy and stable framework of major-country relationship; opening up a new situation in China's relations with developing countries and providing practical foreign aid; adhering to the values of friendship, justice and shared interests on diplomatic work, conscientiously performing the mission of diplomacy of working for the people, and effectively safeguarding China's positive international image and protecting its overseas interests; playing the role of a responsible major-country, contributing Chinese wisdom to the improvement of global governance and participating in the efforts to solve various global problems more constructively; adhering to the basic policy of opening to the outside world and creating an even more comprehensive, in-depth and diversified model of foreign relations in such major international cooperation projects as the Belt and Road Initiative. "The world is so big and faces so many problems, and the international community wants to hear China's voice and see China's solutions. China cannot be absent."[36] On the basis of the idea of building a community of shared future for mankind, China has blazed a trail of major-country diplomacy with Chinese characteristics, greatly enhanced China's international status. "A great era calls for great vision,

---

36 President Xi Jinping sent the New Year message for 2016. People's Daily. 2016-01-01(1).

which in turn requires great wisdom."[37] The idea of building a community of shared future for mankind has a profound strategic vision and distinctive Chinese characteristics, contains the common value of all mankind, and has gained wide support and positive response from all countries in the world, especially the developing countries. With the rise of its national strength, China's advocacy and practice of building a community of shared future for mankind will have a wider range of international influence. The theoretical connotations of building this community will also be enriched and developed, further highlight its great significance.

37   Xi J P. Seek sustained development and fulfill the Asia-Pacific dream: address to the APEC CEO Summit. People's Daily. 2014-11-10 (2).

Chapter 2

Establishing a New Model of International Relations Featuring Win-Win Cooperation

The establishment of a new type of international relations featuring win-win cooperation is a blueprint for China to comply with the requirements of the times to maintain the equal dignity of all countries and peoples , and to share the fruits of both development and security assurance. This blueprint and the concept of building a community of shared future for mankind draw on and enrich each other. Both are about cooperation and win-win progress; both embody China's aspiration to make world a better place. China's tireless pursuit of this goal.

The new type of international relations is about what kind of state-to-state relations China wishes to build, and the community of shared future is about what kind of world China hopes to create. The latter has profound political, economic, security, cultural and ecological dimensions. [1]

A community of shared future for mankind is the goal of the new type of international relations. The new type of international relations featuring win-win cooperation elaborates on China's principled position on the international situations in recent years, and manifests China's wishes and aspirations as a responsible major country.

---

1 WANG Y. A year of flying colors for pursuing major-country diplomacy with Chinese characteristics. International studies. 2016 (1).

1. The proposition and connotations of a new model of international relations

The present era sees unprecedentedly close interdependence and growing interest reciprocality between countries. The challenges facing world peace and development are increasingly global, comprehensive and long lasting, and require coordinated action by all countries. In March 2013, President Xi Jinping pointed out in his speech at the Moscow Institute of International Relations that, in the face of the profound changes in the international situation and the common demands of the rest of the world,

> To keep up with the times, we cannot have ourselves physically living in the 21st century, but with a mindset belonging to the past, stalled in the old days of colonialism, and constrained by zero-sum Cold War mentality. The world community should jointly push for the building of a new type of international relations with win-win cooperation as the core, and people of all nations should combine their efforts to safeguard world peace and promote common development.[2]

This is the first time for the new concept of international relations with win-win cooperation as the core was clearly put forward. In November 2014, General Secretary Xi Jinping stressed at the Central Conference on Work Relating to Foreign Affairs:

> We should adhere to win-win cooperation and promote a new type of international relations featuring win-win cooperation. We should continue to follow the win-win strategy of opening-up and a win-win approach in every aspect of our external relations, including the political, economic, security and cultural fields.[3]

The idea of building a new type of international relations featuring win-win cooperation has been established as the framework principles of China's diplomacy. In September 2015, when attending the Series of Summits marking the 70th Anniversary of the United Nations, President Xi Jinping further elaborated on the new concept of international relations and pointed out that the idea of a new type of international relations follows and carries forward the purposes and principles of the UN Charter.

---

2   XI J P. The governance of China. Beijing: Foreign Languages Press. 2014: 273.
3   The central conference on work relating to foreign affairs was held in Beijing. People's Daily. 2014-11-3O (1).

Win-win cooperation is the core of the new concept of international relations, and also a concept with distinctive features of the times with Chinese characteristics. Cooperation is the means, which should replace confrontation; win-win result is the goal, which should replace monopoly. The objective requirements of economic globalization bind all countries closely together, and many of the global challenges facing mankind cannot be solved by one country alone. Their solution lies solely in cooperation. Therefore, all countries need to develop a sense of community, abandon old ideas of international relations as the zero-sum game and winner-take-all mind sets that are inconsistent with the trends of the times. Cooperation can create peace, promote development, and replace zero-sum development with interdependent win-win development. Win-win cooperation includes not only the pursuit of interests, but also the pursuit of common development, emphasizing the morality and responsibility that comes along with interests. The concept of win-win cooperation is not based on the weakening of national sovereignty, but sets the latter as a prerequisite respecting the equality, independence and inviolability of sovereign states. It holds that all countries are equal, regardless of their size, strength and wealth, that cooperation is established on the balanced basis of sovereign states pursuing their own interests and fulfilling their international obligations, and that "win-win" means to achieve the common development of both their own interests and the common interests of mankind. Only by realizing the common development of all countries and letting more people share the fruits of development can there be a solid foundation and effective guarantee for world peace, and the development of all countries be sustained.

The new type of international relations featuring win-win cooperation is not solely applicable to the economic field. The concept of win-win cooperation is intrinsically consistent with the principles in the UN Charter. It is the only approach to new international relations, widely applicable to political, safety and cultural areas. In terms of politics, win-win cooperation means to have dialogue instead of confrontation, and to establish partnership instead of alignment. As President Xi Jinping said, "partners include both those who cherish the same ideals and follow the same path as ours and those who seek common ground while reserving differences from ours."[4] China advocates re-

---

4   XI J P. Deepening partnership and promoting common prosperity of the Asia-Pacific region: keynote speech at Asia-Pacific Economic Cooperation Economic Leaders' Meeting. People's Daily. 2016-11-21 (3).

spect for each country's independent choice of foreign policy in international relations and for the social system and development path chosen by each country. It opposes the big bullying the small or the strong bullying the weak. In terms of security, win-win cooperation means to establish the concepts of common security, cooperation and security, comprehensive security and sustainable security, and to adhere to the peaceful resolution of disputes between countries through dialogue and consultation, as opposed to the frequent use of force or threat of force, opening up a new, shared and win-win result to security by joint efforts from all countries. In terms of culture, win-win cooperation means to develop harmoniously through mutual appreciation, mutual inclusiveness and mutual learning, to put an end to cultural chauvinism and cultural hegemonism, to draw on the wisdom of different cultures, to share the fruits of human civilization, and to promote human progress. In short, zero-sum mindset is out of date; the world must take a harmonious, cooperative and win-win new path. The idea of win-win cooperation has brought about new perspectives on solving the differences in international relations, conforming to the universal aspirations of the international community and becoming the core of building a new type of international relations.

The new model of international relations featuring win-win cooperation is not a castle in the air, but is based on the diplomatic practice and experience since China's reform and opening-up. For more than 30 years, China has explored a path different from that of the rise of big countries in history and created a unique model of synergistic interplay between its own development and that of world peace. With this model, "we can both promote China's domestic development and open the country wider to the outside world and advance both China's development and the development of the world as a whole, as well as the interests of both the Chinese people and other peoples."[5] For a long time, China has adhered to cooperation with other countries in the world. China has not resorted to means of direct confrontation and conflict even in the unfair, unjustified international systems dominated by the Western countries, but has made efforts to participate in them and planned to reform them with its own enhanced strength in a gradual manner instead. "What China pursues is common development, which means we are aiming for a better life for the Chinese people and for

---

5　XI J P. The governance of China. Beijing: Foreign Languages Press. 2014: 248.

the peoples of other countries."[6] China's great achievements have created opportunities for the economic growth of all countries in the world and set a good example for the success of developing countries. However, some countries still have little trust in China's development out of the considerations of geopolitical, ideological, strategic competition and other factors, and allow the spread of such ill-founded notions as the "China threat" --"a country is bound to seek hegemony when it grows in strength" into the international community. In this sense, China's proposition of establishing a new international relations featuring win-win cooperation is intended to increase international trust and clear up doubts, and to take the initiative to show its position and commitment to the world: China has successfully explored a pathway of peaceful development; it is confident in finding a new pathway of win-win cooperation with all countries in the world.

2. Peace, development, cooperation and win-win result becoming the trend of the times

Each stage of history has a specific theme. The so-called theme of the times is determined by the fundamental contradictions of the historical stage, referring to global and strategic issues. With the shifts in the balance of power and correlations between the world's fundamentally contradictory forces, the theme of the times will shift too. The correct understanding of the theme of the times is not only a major theoretical issue, but also an essential and practical issue to a country's overall development strategy.

After the Third Plenary Session of the 11th CPC Central Committee, Comrade Deng Xiaoping conducted a comprehensive, thorough and scientific analysis and forward-looking strategic assessment on the themes of the times that aiming at maintaining the overall situation of the reform and opening-up and socialist modernization, with a view of planning a favorable international environment for China's future. He profoundly observed that, peace and development are the two major themes of the times. From the middle 1980s, Comrade Deng Xiaoping had repeatedly pointed out, "currently the world is confronted by many issues, two of which are overriding: one is the peace issue, the other is the North-South issue."[7]

---

6   Ibid. 315.
7   DENG X P. Selected works of Deng Xiaoping: Vol.:1. Beijing: People's Publishing House. 1993: 96.

Now the really important issues in the world, which are of global strategic significance, are the issue of peace, economy and development. The peace issue exists between the East and the West, and development issue exists between the North and the South. To sum it up, they are the East -West issue and the North South issue.[8]

In 1992, the 14th National Congress of the CPC raised peace and development to the height of the themes of the times. In 2007, the 17th National Congress of the CPC reaffirmed, "peace and development remain the main themes of the present era, and pursuit of peace, development and cooperation have become an irresistible trend of the times."[9] In 2012, the 18th National Congress of the CPC stressed again that "peace and development remain the underlying trends of our times"[10], and further declared that "China will continue to hold high the banner of peace, development, cooperation and mutual benefit and strive to uphold world peace and promote common development."[11]

In the face of the ever-changing world, China clearly grasps the themes of peace and development, quickly implements the strategy of opening to the outside world, continuously reinforces the concept of cooperation, and strengthens its pragmatic and friendly cooperation with all countries in the world to meet the challenges of global problems.

It has been seeking the meeting point of the interests of all sides and committed to achieving win-win situations. General Secretary Xi Jinping, on the basis of adhering to the strategic judgments on the themes of the times, deepens the understanding of the world trends and the trends of the times. He said: "it is a world where peace, development, cooperation and mutual benefit have become the trend of the times."[12] This judgement puts forward the idea of win-win cooperation while emphasizing the themes of peace and development. It highly summarizes the basic trends and characteristics

---

8   DENG X P. Selected works of Deng Xiaoping, Vol. 3. Beijing, People's Publishing House. 1993: 105.

9   HU J T. Hold high the great banner of socialism with Chinese characteristics and strive for new victories in building a moderately prosperous society in all respects: report to the 17th National Congress of the Communist Party of China. People's Daily. 2007-10-25.

10 HU J T. Firmly march on the path of socialism with Chinese characteristics and strive to complete the building of a moderately prosperous society in all respects: report to the 18th National Congress of the Communist Party of China. People's Daily. 2012-11-18.

11 Ibid.

12 XI J P. The governance of China. Beijing: Foreign Languages Press. 2014: 272.

of the current development in international relations, enriches China's view of the times in this new era, and is of great significance to the exploration of the path of major-country diplomacy with Chinese characteristics. The judgment that peace, development, cooperation and win-win have become the trend of the times has profound ideological connotations and important practical significance. Since the beginning of the 21st century, uncertainties affecting world peace and development have been increasing, traditional security threats and non-traditional security threats have been intertwined, regional conflicts have been continuous, world economic growth has been unstable, trade protectionism has risen, development is uneven, and the North-South gap continues to widen. However, the basic situation of the world's overall peace has not changed; the direction of economic globalization has not changed. The maintenance of world peace and the promotion of common development are still the common aspirations of the peoples of the world. Peace is a prerequisite for development, and development is an important guarantee of peace. Seeking development in peace and promoting peace in development is the only way for human society to move towards a better future. At the same time, with deepening interdependence, countries increasingly rise and fall together. Countries may differ in culture, faith and system, but win-win cooperation is the greatest common divisor, which should be the only rational choice in dealing with international relations. Cooperation is the necessary path to win-win result, and win-win result the goal of cooperation. Increasing win-win situations through cooperation and deepening cooperation in win-win situations will enable countries to work together to solve the major issues of world peace, international development and human progress.

Peace, development, cooperation and win-win result have become the trend of the times. This judgment creates conditions for the realization of the Chinese Dream of the great rejuvenation of the Chinese nation. The realization of the Chinese Dream cannot be fulfilled without the strategic opportunity when peace, development, cooperation and win-win result have become the trend of the times. The 16th "National Congress of the CPC once pointed out that the first 20 years of the 21st century would be an important strategic opportunity for China that must be firmly grasped and made the best use of. Opportunity refers to the favorable time and space for an action. A country's strategic opportunities refer to the favorable times, conditions and factors that can have a positive impact on the country's overall and long-term development. The 18th National Congress of the CPC reaffirmed: "An examination of both the current international and domestic environments shows that China remains in an important period of strategic opportunities for its development, a period in which much can be achieved."[13] The world should be peaceful, the country should be developed, the society should progress, and the economy should be prosperous. These values have become common aspirations of the peoples around the world, creating a stable and sustained period of strategic opportunities for the realization of the Chinese Dream.

> The Chinese Dream is a dream of peace, development, cooperation and win-win result, which is closely related to the beautiful dreams of all peoples of the world. The Chinese people are willing to work together with all peoples of the world, supporting each other and helping each other in the process of realizing their individual dreams.[14]

Without peace, China and the world at large cannot develop smoothly; without development, neither China nor the world as a whole can enjoy enduring peace; without win-win cooperation, mankind will not see a beautiful future. The Chinese Dream benefits both the Chinese people and peoples around the world. What the realization of the Chinese Dream brings to the world is peace and opportunity instead of turbulence and threat.

This judgment that peace, development, cooperation and win-win result have become the trend of the times provides a theoretical premise for the establishment of a new type of international relations featuring win-win cooperation.

Peace is the common ground for building a new type of international relations. "Peace is the ever-lasting wish of our people. Peace, like air and sunshine, is hardly noticed when people are benefiting from it. But none of us can live without it."[15] The Chinese nation has been peace-loving throughout history. Hegemony or militarism is simply not in the genes of the Chinese.

---

13   HU J T. Firmly march on the path of socialism with Chinese characteristics and strive to complete the building of a moderately prosperous society in all respects: report to the 18th National Congress of the Communist Party of China. People's Daily. 2012-11-18.
14   The Publicity Department of the CPC Central Committee. General Secretary Xi Jinping's series of important remarks (2016 edition). Beijing: Xuexi Publishing House. 2016: 15-16.
15   XI J P. The governance of China. Beijing: Foreign Languages Press. 2014: 331.

Adherence to an independent foreign policy of peace is the basis of China's foreign relations. In the face of the ever-changing international situation, China, as a responsible major country, has always been a strong supporter of world peace and a firm proponent of the trends of the times.

Development is the fundamental pathway to build a new type of international relations. China is committed to promoting the common development of all countries in the world and being a contributor to global development. In September 2015, President Xi Jinping presented a new point of view on Chinese development in the speech at the United Nations Sustainable Development Summit, which states that countries should "collectively follow an equitable, open, comprehensive and innovation-driven development path, and strive to achieve common development."[16] Development must be fair and development opportunities must be made more equal for all countries. It is not true development if one country develops but other countries do not, or if some countries develop while others do not. Development must be open, so that all countries can learn from each other's development experience and share the fruits of development. Development must be comprehensive, and all countries should strive to achieve economically, socially and environmentally coordinated development, so that the harmony between the man and the society and between the man and the nature will be achieved. Development must be innovative, with reform and innovation stimulating mankind's potentials, so that new core competitiveness will be cultivated.

Cooperation is the only way to build a new type of international relations. Peaceful development is inseparable from cooperation. Only by cooperation can we safeguard world peace, and only by cooperation can we promote common development. China has long maintained the development of friendly cooperative relations with all countries on the basis of the Five Principles of Peaceful Coexistence. In March 2015, when President Xi Jinping attended the Asian-African leaders' meeting, he put forward the concept of cooperation featuring deepening Asia-Africa cooperation, expanding South-South cooperation and promoting North-South cooperation, which further strengthened China's friendly and cooperative relations with all countries in the world.

Win-win result is the essential requirement of building a new type of

---

16   Speeches by Xi Jinping at the Series of Summits Marking the 70th Anniversary of the United Nations. Beijing: People's Publishing House. 2015: 2.

international relations. The significance of win-win concept is to break through the "zero-sum game" mindset and transcend the historical mistakes that "a country is bound to seek hegemony when it grows in strength".

The new mechanisms and initiatives launched by China are not intended to reinvent the wheels or target any other country. Rather, they aim to complement and improve the current international mechanisms to achieve win-win cooperation and common development. China's opening drive is not a one-man show. Rather, it is an invitation open to all. It is a pursuit not to establish China's own sphere of influence, but to support common development of all countries. It is meant to build not China's own backyard garden, but a garden shared by all countries. [17]

Holding high the banner of the trend of the times of "peace, development, cooperation and win-win result", China has made a series of important achievements in practicing major-country diplomacy with Chinese characteristics, which have important guiding significance for building a new type of international relations featuring win-win cooperation.

3. Firmly and unswervingly following the path of peaceful development

Peaceful development is a new way of development in which peace and development are interdependent, internal and foreign affairs are unified, and the national interests of one country are closely integrated with the common interests of mankind. It is a great initiative in the history of international relations and a great progress in the development of the human society. Adherence to the path of peaceful development is not only written in the reports of the 17th and 18th National Congresses of the CPC, but also included in the Constitution of the CPC, becoming the national will, entering the national development plans and major policies, and implemented in a wide range of practice in China's development process. Since the 18th National Congress of the CPC, General Secretary Xi Jinping has repeatedly made comprehensive, profound and incisive expositions on the major issue of China's peaceful development, which has further enriched the connotation of peaceful development. He said,

China made the solemn declaration to the world long ago that China is

____

17   XI J P. A new starting point for China's development, a new blueprint for global growth: keynote speech at the opening ceremony of the B 20 Summit. People's Daily. 2016-09-04.

committed to pursuing peaceful development. It strives to develop itself by upholding world peace and maintain world peace through its development. Pursuing peaceful development is China's response to international concern about the direction of China's development. Moreover, it demonstrates the Chinese people's confidence and commitment to realize its development.[18]

China's pursuit of peaceful development is not an act of expediency, still less diplomatic rhetoric. Rather, it is China's strategic choice and solemn commitment, with profound historical inevitability and practical necessity. Taking the path of peaceful development is the inheritance and development of the fine cultural tradition of the Chinese nation and the inevitable conclusion the Chinese people have drawn from their sufferings from modern times. Peaceful development was hard-won, gradually formed during the continuous exploration and practice after the founding of the New China in 1949, especially after the reform and opening-up. In the long run, China put forward and adhered to the Five Principles of Peaceful Coexistence, established and pursued an independent diplomatic policy of peace, and made a commitment to the world that China would never seek hegemony and never engage in expansion. With the rapid rise of China, the international community has introduced different kinds of theories on the "China threat" or "a country is bound to seek hegemony when it grows in strength", claiming that China will inevitably take the historical road of aggression and expansion like the Western powers did. By clearly committing itself to peaceful development, China is determined to blaze a new way to achieve national development and rejuvenation peacefully. More than 30 years of reform and opening up experience has proved that peaceful development conforms to the historical trends, that it is in line with both China's fundamental interests and the interests of the whole world, and there is no reason to change it. The 18th National Congress of the CPC put forward the "Two Centenary Goals", and after that China raised the Chinese Dream, i. e. the goal of realizing the great rejuvenation of the Chinese nation. Although China has become the world's second largest economy, its per capita level is still lagging behind. China is still the largest developing country in the world. The state of being in unbalanced, uncoordinated and unsustainable development in China will last for quite a long time. To achieve the "Two Centenary Goals" and Chinese Dream, it is necessary for China to continue

---

18　XI J P. The governance of China. Beijing: Foreign Languages Press. 2014: 265.

to stand firm in the path of peaceful development and to promote its own peaceful development into a new historical stage. Therefore, "China's determination and wish of following the path of peaceful development will never be shaken by anyone, anything for any reason."[19]

General Secretary Xi Jinping relates the overall consideration of both domestic and international situations to achieving peaceful development, pointing out the direction for China to adhere to the peaceful development.

> We should, under the guidance of Deng Xiaoping Theory, the important thought of the Three Represents and the Scientific Outlook on Development, enhance our strategic thinking and confidence, and better balance China's overall domestic and international interests. We should pursue mutually beneficial development featuring openness and cooperation, develop China by securing a peaceful international environment and, at the same time, uphold and promote world peace through our own development. We should continuously improve China's overall national strength, make sure that the people share the benefits of peaceful development, and consolidate the material and social foundations for pursuing peaceful development.[20]

Pursuing peaceful development depends not only on China's subjective will, but also on whether China can obtain the internal and external conditions for peaceful development. China's path of peaceful development is formed on the basis of grasping the general trends of the world and l earning the experience and lessons from its own reform and opening-up. To get an even better understanding of the internal and external situations, it is especially necessary to grasp the direction of development of the relation between international and domestic situations, to create conditions for development out of the complementary advantages of resources, to master the overall situation of development through the comprehensive interaction between international and domestic factors.

> A prosperous and stable world provides China with opportunities, and China's developmental so offers an opportunity for the world as a whole. Whether we will succeed in our pursuit of peaceful development to a large extent hinges on whether we can turn opportunities of the rest of the world into China's opportunities and China's opportunities into those for the rest of

19   XI J P. Work together to promote openness, inclusiveness and peaceful development: speech at dinner hosted by the lord mayor of the city of London. People's Daily. 2015-10-23.
20   XI J P. The governance of China. Beijing: Foreign Languages Press. 2014: 247.

the world so that China and other countries can engage in sound interactions and make mutually beneficial progress. [21]

General Secretary Xi Jinping clarified the relationship between maintaining China's core interests and pursuing peaceful development, pointed out that China has the bottom line in its pursuit of peaceful development.

> While pursuing peaceful development, we will never sacrifice our legitimate rights and interests or China's core interests. No foreign country should expect China to trade off its core interests or swallow bitter fruit that undermines China's sovereignty, security or development interests. China is pursuing peaceful development, and so are other countries. This is the sure way for all the countries in the world to seek common development and peaceful coexistence. [22]

China's pursuit of peaceful development will not be at the expense of its own national interests, and adherence to the path of peaceful development is neither absolute nor unconditional. Peace is not spontaneous, but is achieved through struggle and safeguard. When China's sovereignty, security and developmental interests arc threatened, it will resolutely use all means to safeguard its core national interests. This is not contradictory to the pursuit of peaceful development, but is internally consistent. Peaceful development is the trend of the times and taking the path of peaceful development is the common responsibility of all countries in the world. Only when more countries have embarked on the road of peaceful development can we achieve long-term peaceful development. To this end, General Secretary Xi Jinping proposed that China should unswervingly stick to peaceful development, extensively and thoroughly publicize China's strategic thinking of peaceful development, and guide the international community to correctly understand and treat China's development. China will never seek development at the expense of any other country's interests, nor will it shift its problems onto others.

For decades, China has always adhered to an independent foreign policy of peace and always followed the path of peaceful development. General Secretary Xi Jinping's new ideas and new judgements on peaceful development will lead China on an increasingly wide road of peaceful development,

---

21   XI J P. The governance of China. Beijing: Foreign Languages Press. 2014: 248.
22   XI J P. The governance of China. Beijing: Foreign Languages Press. 2014: 249.

realize the Chinese Dream of the great rejuvenation of the Chinese nation soon.

4 . Maintaining China's friendly relations with neighborhood countries

Neighborhood areas are given priority in China's diplomacy. Consolidating and expanding China's good-neighborly and friendly relations with those countries and regions is the foothold of China's peaceful development and a demonstration area for practicing the new type of international relations. China is the major country with the most complex surrounding environments, bordering 14 neighboring countries on land, 6 countries across the seas, and 9 countries that do not border but are close neighbors. China's peace and stability, development and prosperity began in the neighborhood, and the changes in relationship between China and the world is first reflected in the changes in the relationship between China and its neighboring countries. "Regions around our borders arc strategically significant to our country in terms of geography, the environment, and relationships."[23] In the world, China and its neighbors are full of vigor and vitality, and show obvious strengths and high potential in development. The region is stable on the whole, and most of its neighbors maintain an amicable relationship geared toward mutual benefit and cooperation with China. However, the surrounding countries are very diversified in history and culture, ethnicity and religion, political system, level of development and other aspects. In recent years, as the relationship between China and its neighboring countries has become even closer and our interests has been more integrated, the surrounding environment has undergone great changes. Some disputes on territorial sovereignty and maritime rights and interests have become conspicuous; new situations have occurred in neighborhood relations. These objective situations require that China's neighborhood diplomacy must keep pace with the times and take the initiative.

At the Boao Forum for Asia Annual Conference in April 2013, President Xi Jinping made it clear, "China will continue to promote friendship and partnership with its neighbors, consolidate friendly ties and deepen mutually beneficial cooperation with them and ensure that its development will bring even greater benefits to its neighbors."[24] In September and October

---

23   XI J P. The governance of China. Beijing: Foreign Languages Press. 2014: 296-297.
24   XI J P. The governance of China. Beijing: Foreign Languages Press. 2014: 332.

2013, President Xi Jinping proposed the concepts of the Belt and Road Initiative in Kazakhstan and Indonesia respectively, making the grand blueprint for comprehensively improving the cooperation between China and its neighboring countries, which received wide and positive responses from those countries. On this basis, in October 2013, the first Seminar on the Work of Neighborhood Diplomacy since the Founding of the New China was held. General Secretary Xi Jinping delivered an important speech to clarify the strategic objectives, basic principles and overall layout of China's neighborhood diplomacy under the new situations. He said,

> China's diplomacy with neighboring countries is driven by and serve the "Two Centenary Goals" and the Chinese Dream of the national rejuvenation. To achieve these strategic aims, we must create and cement friendly relations and further mutually beneficial cooperation with neighboring countries, maintain and make the best use of the strategic opportunities we now enjoy, and safeguard China's state sovereignty, national security, and development interests. Together we must strive to build more amicable political relationships and closer economic ties, to further security cooperation and to encourage more cultural and people-to-people exchanges with neighboring countries.[25]

The importance of neighborhood diplomacy in the overall situation of China's diplomacy has been significantly strengthened.

General Secretary Xi Jinping emphasized, "China's fundamental policy of diplomacy with neighboring countries is to treat them as friends and partners, to make them feel secure and to support their development. This policy is characterized by friendship, sincerity, reciprocity and inclusiveness.[26] Friendship means to consolidate the friendly feelings brought by our geographical nearness and interpersonal affinity; sincerity means to treat neighboring countries with sincerity and to get along with them well; reciprocity means to implement the concept of cooperation for the benefit of the neighborhood, for mutual benefit and win-win result; inclusiveness means to display our broad mind as a major country characterized by openness and inclusiveness and seeking common ground while reserving differences. General Secretary Xi Jinping pointed out,

> Friendship is a consistent principle of China's diplomacy with its neighbors. In adherence to this principle, we need to help neighbors in times of

---

25   XI J P. The governance of China. Beijing: Foreign Languages Press. 2014: 297.
26   Ibid.

crises, treat them as equals, visit them frequently, and take actions that will win us support and friendship. In response, we hope that neighboring countries will be well inclined towards us, and we hope that China will have a stronger affinity with them, and that our appeal and our influence will grow. We must treat neighbors with sincerity and cultivate them as friends and partners. We should cooperate with our neighbors on the basis of reciprocity, create a closer network of common interests, and better integrate China's interests with theirs, so that they can benefit from China's development and China can benefit and gain support from theirs. We should advocate inclusiveness, stressing that there is enough room in the Asia Pacific region for all countries to develop, and promoting regional cooperation with an open mind and enthusiasm. We must embrace and practice these ideas, so that they will become the shared beliefs and norms of conduct for the whole region.[27]

General Secretary Xi Jinping's elaboration on the basic policy of neighborhood diplomacy elevates the relationship between China and neighboring countries to the moral and emotional level, reflecting China's good wishes and non-zero-sum new mentality to seek common development of both China and its neighboring countries, showing China's affinity and self confidence in welcoming the neighboring countries and their peoples to share China's reform and opening-up dividend. While focusing on strengthening economic relations with its neighbors, China has also made great efforts to improve the quality of its relations with them, creating the comprehensive relationship of economic interdependency, mutual trust in national security and close cultural relations, and promoting further deepening of the win-win situation of mutual benefit between China and its neighbors.

In Northeast Asia, China firmly promotes the denuclearization of the Korean Peninsula, firmly upholds its legitimate interests and strategic security environment, and insists on resolving the nuclear issue through dialogues and negotiations to maintain peace and stability on the Korean peninsula. In the spirit of "taking history as a mirror, looking forward into the future", China promotes China-Japanese relations in the right direction. China has promoted China-Mongolia relations to a comprehensive strategic partnership. China and Southeast Asia are connected by mountains and rivers, and China stands firm in establishing friendly cooperation with ASEAN, in supporting the development and building of the ASEAN

---

27   XI J P. The governance of China. Beijing: Foreign Languages Press. 2014: 297-298.

community, and supporting ASEAN's leading role in regional cooperation in the East Asia. China is facing a rare opportunity for the development of relations with Central Asian countries. It hopes to further enhance mutual trust, consolidate friendship and strengthen cooperation with the Central Asian countries, so as to promote the common development and prosperity and create well-being for peoples of both sides. China" will never interfere in the internal affairs of Central Asian countries. China does not seek to dominate regional affairs or establish any sphere of influence."[28] China and South Asian countries are important partners. China is willing to live in harmony with the countries of the South Asia and is willing to contribute to the development of the region." China's cooperation with the South Asia, like a massive treasure long-awaited to be unearthed, promises great prospects for us."[29] India is the largest country in the South Asia. China is ready to work together with India and make greater contribution to the development of the region so that the three billion people living on both sides of the Himalayas will enjoy peace, friendship, stability and prosperity. Pakistan and China have been good friends, good neighbors, good partners and good brothers. China-Pakistan relations have been promoted to all-weather strategic partnership." By all weather, we mean that our two countries will always move ahead together rain or shine. This description of China-Pakistan partnership is the most appropriate one, as it vividly defines the all weather friendship and all-round cooperation between China and Pakistan."[30]

Since the 18th National Congress of the CPC, General Secretary Xi Jinping has left footprints in all neighboring countries and regions, and China's radiating influence has been spreading, and neighborhood diplomatic layout has become increasingly mature. "China has received support from its neighbors in its development endeavors, and China's development, in turn, has benefited its neighbors. China hopes that its own development and that of its neighbors will complement each other, and China welcomes its neighbors to board the fast train of China's development so that they

28 XI J P. The governance of China. Beijing: Foreign Languages Press. 2014: 288.
29 XI J P. In joint pursuit of a dream of national rejuvenation: speech at the Indian Council of World Affairs. People's Daily. 2014-09-19.
30 XI J P. Building a China-Pakistan community of shared destiny to pursue closer win-win cooperation: speech at the Parliament of Pakistan. People's Daily. 2015-04-22.

can share more from China's development."[31] Focusing on the realistic and long-term needs of the common development of both China and its neigh boring countries, China is actively promoting the construction of various mechanisms in the neighborhood hy supporting the development of the Shanghai Cooperation Organization (SCO), implementing the Belt and Road Initiative, constructing the Bangladesh-China-India-Myanmar Economic Corridor and the China-Pakistan Economic Corridor, updating China-ASEAN Free Trade Area, planning and building the AIIB, promoting regional comprehensive economic partnership and the negotiations on free trade areas between China, Japan and the Republic of Korea (ROK), and starting the Lancang-Mekong River cooperation mechanism. China and the neighboring countries have increasingly become a multi-level community of shared future.

At present, there are still many unstable and uncertain factors in our neighborhood that disturb China's peaceful development. Local hot spots and sensitive issues pack there, causing the regional security cooperation to lag far behind economic cooperation. China is committed to properly solve the hot issues in the region, playing a constructive role in promoting the stability of the surrounding situation. China has firmly safeguarded its territorial sovereignty and legitimate maritime rights and interests in respect of territorial sovereignty problems left over by history and issues over maritime rights and interests. At the same time, China advocates finding proper solutions through dialogues and negotiations on the basis of full respect for historical facts and the international law, and objects to actions that heating up and complicating the issues. For the problems that cannot be solved for the moment, China advocates shelving disputes, developing jointly, and narrowing differences through dialogue and cooperation so that creating conditions for the resolution of those problems in the future." As circumstances evolve, diplomacy with neighboring countries requires us to analyze and deal with issues strategically, improve our capabilities in planning and implementation, and promote every aspect of this diplomacy."[32] Under the guidance of Xi Jinping's new thought on neighborhood diplomacy, China and its neighbors have opened up a new situation of neighborhood

---

31 XI J P. Forging a strong partnership to enhance prosperity of Asia: speech at the National University of Singapore. People's Daily. 2015-11-07.
32 XI J P. The governance of China. Beijing: Foreign Languages Press. 2014: 298.

diplomacy and worked together to forge a new type of international relations in the neighboring areas.

5. Building a new model of major-country relations

Major countries are important forces that affect world peace and development. It is the inherent logic of the Western theory of international relations that the relationship between major countries, especially between the emerging major powers and the existing powers, will evolve from competition to confrontation and even conflict, falling into the so-called "Thucydides Trap". As the most important developing country today, China does not agree with the so-called historical destiny, but puts forward a new concept of building a new model of major-country relations, and strives to break that so-called law of major-country relations. The Report of the 18th National Congress of the CPC proposed: "we will strive to establish a new type of relations of long-term stability and sound growth with other major countries."[33] In June 2013, when President Xi Jinping met with then US President Barack Obama at the Annenberg Estate, he proposed to build a new type of major-country relationship featuring non-conflict, mutual respect and win-win cooperation: "China and the US should and can build a new model of relationship different from the historical clashes and confrontations between major powers, given the rapid economic globalization and the need for all countries in the world to work together."[34] setting the direction for the future development of China-US bilateral relations. In November 2014, General Secretary Xi Jinping stressed at the Central Conference on Work Relating to Foreign Affairs, "we should manage well relations with other major countries, build a sound and stable framework of major-country relations, and expand cooperation with other major developing countries."[35] Although the new concept of building a new model of major country relations is proposed for China-US relations, its connotation also applies to other major-country relations. Different from the old

---

33 HU J T. Firmly march on the path of socialism with Chinese characteristics and strive to complete the building of a moderately prosperous society in all respects: report to the 18th National Congress of the CPC. People's Daily. 2012-11-18.
34 XI J P. The governance of China. Beijing: Foreign Languages Press. 2014: 279.
35 The central conference on work relating to foreign affairs was held in Beijing. People's Daily. 2014-11-30.

mentality that the relationship between major countries is either alliance or confrontation, the new model of major-country relations takes the responsibility for safeguarding world peace and the common interests of mankind as its prerequisite, equality and mutual trust, cooperation and win-win result as its main feature. The confidence to build a new model of major-country relations lies in the fact that today's world is very different from what it was. Globalization has created such an interest connection between all countries that they rise and fall together, which has not only greatly weakened the will of the confrontation between the major countries, but also significantly reduced the risk of conflicts and wars. The construction of a new model of major-country relations is an important part of the new type of international relations featuring win-win cooperation, which is of great significance to China's adherence to the path of peaceful development.

Russia is the China's largest neighbor. Having a wide range of common interests, the two countries are good neighbors, good partners and good friends. China and Russia have established a comprehensive strategic partnership of coordination featuring mutual trust, mutual support, common prosperity and friendship from generation to generation. As President Xi Jinping pointed out,

> The relationship between China and Russia is one of the most important bilateral relationships in the world. It is also the best relationship between major countries. A strong and high performance relationship like this not only serves the interests of our two countries but also provides an important safe guard for maintaining international strategic balance as well as peace and stability in the world.[36]

Both countries regard each other as the priority in their diplomatic relations. They live in harmony, treat each other equally, take concrete actions to firmly support each other on respective core interests, on respective development and rejuvenation, and on following the development paths suited to respective national conditions, and establish a high degree of political mutual trust. Both countries regard each other as an opportunity for their own development. They firmly support each other on doing a good job with respective affairs and endeavors, and on seeking respective development growth, and on offering and seeking mutual assistance, and are committed

---

36   XI J P. The governance of China. Beijing: Foreign Languages Press. 2014: 275.

to common development to achieve common prosperity. The two countries have established a comprehensive mechanism for high-level exchanges for prompt close communication, in-depth consultation and frank exchange of views on major issues of mutual concern, in order to resolve the difficulties and problems in cooperation and ensure that their bilateral relations are running on a high level with high efficiency. Based on the win-win cooperation, the two countries have carried out mutually beneficial economic cooperation. The areas of their cooperation range from basic trade to investment, financing, energy, aviation, high-tech, high-speed train, agriculture and other fields. The forms of their cooperation developed from the simple buyer-seller relationship to joint research and development and joint production. The level of their cooperation increases from border trade to strategic large projects. They deeply integrate the economic interests of both countries. China-Russia people-to-people and cultural exchanges flourish, increasing the mutual favor and the traditional friendship between the two peoples. The two countries closely coordinate and cooperate in international and regional affairs, support each other in the UN, the SCO, the BRICS, the G20 and other international and regional organizations, and jointly promote the political settlement process of international and regional hot issues, improve the global governance system and become key factors and constructive forces to promote international peace and stability. China-Russia comprehensive strategic partnership of coordination has gone far beyond the category of bilateral relations and has become a paragon of the new model of major-country relations.

China-US relations are the most complicated bilateral relations in the world today and occupy a particularly important position in China's diplomatic layout. China and the US account for one third of the world's economy, one quarter of the world's population, and one fifth of the world's total trade. Building a new type of major-country relations, upholding non-conflict and non-confrontation, mutual respect and win-win cooperation, are the common aspirations of the two peoples and the international community, and is in line with the trends of the times, which reflects the two countries' resolution to break the traditional model of major-power conflict and confrontation as well as their political commitment to creating a new model of developing major-country relations. For China and the US to build a new type of major-power relations, non-conflict and non-confrontation is the necessary prerequisite, mutual respect the basic principle, and win-win cooperation is the only way." The broad Pacific Ocean is vast enough to embrace the two major countries of China and the US."[37] As the world's largest developing country and the largest developed country, China-US cooperation sees broad prospects. Either in developing their respective national economy, or in promoting the global economic stability and recovery; either in handling international and regional hot issues, or in meeting a variety of global challenges, the two countries have huge common interests and a solid foundation for cooperation. Win-win cooperation is the only right choice for their bilateral relations.

> The building of a new model of major-country relations between China and the US is unprecedented, but it will be faithfully carried out by the two sides. China and the US should work together to push forward the new model of major-country relations by creating dialogues, fostering mutual trust, promoting cooperation and preventing disputes.[38]

China and the US have different national conditions. Their histories and cultures, development paths, social systems, people's demands are not the same, and it is difficult for them to avoid differences in opinion. The two sides should understand each other, handle differences with a broad mind and control differences with positive measures." There is no such thing as the so called' Thucydides Trap' in the world. But if major countries keep making the mistakes of strategic miscalculation, they will possibly create such traps for themselves."[39] The differences between the two countries should not be the source of suspicion or even friction, but should become the motivation for seeking common ground while reserving differences, aggregating similarities and resolving differences, and common improvement. The two countries should follow the order of priorities and properly deal with differences one by one, and gradually establish a habit of dialogue and negotiation in settling problems. With good cooperation, China and the US can become ballast stones in global stability and boosters of world peace. As the strategic significance and global influence of China-US bilateral

---

37   Xi Jinping meets with the Visiting US Secretary of State John Kerry. People's Daily. 2011-04-14.
38   XI J P. The governance of China. Beijing: Foreign Languages Press. 2014: 280.
39   XI J P. Speech at the welcoming dinner jointly hosted by Washington State Government and Friendly Organizations in the United States. People's Daily. 2015-09-24.

relations become increasingly prominent, the two countries should have a sense of historical depth and a vision for the future when managing their relations, and constantly give new meanings and impetus to China-US relations.

Europe is an important driving force of multipolarization in the world. The all-round cooperation between China and the EU is an important basis for China to promote the new type of international relations." As the largest developing country and the largest union of developed countries, China and the EU are the two forces to safeguard world peace. As two important economics in the world, China and the EU are two major markets for promoting common development. As important birthplaces of the Eastern and Western cultures, China and the EU are two civilizations that have promoted human progress."[40] In November 2013, China and the EU formulated the China-EU 2020 Strategic Agenda for Cooperation, which defines the common goals of China-EU cooperation in areas such as peace and security, prosperity, sustainable development and people-to-people exchanges. The two sides agreed to use the annual summit as a strategic guide to their relationship, and to fully implement the Strategic Agenda through the three pillars directly underpinning the summit, namely, the Annual High Level Strategic Dialogue, the Annual High Level Economic and Trade Dialogue, and the bi-annual High Level People-to-People Dialogue. In 2014, when President Xi Jinping visited Europe, he proposed, "we need to build four bridges for peace, growth, reform and progress of civilization, so that the China-EU comprehensive strategic partnership will take on even greater global significance."[41] This initiative has received a positive response from the EU and European countries, and China and the EU have seen deeper mutual trust, stronger partnership and a wider range of cooperation. China and Central-Eastern European countries' "16+1" format cooperation is an important part of China-EU relations.

---

40 Xi Jinping meets with European Council President Herman Van Rompuy and European Commission President Jose Manuel Barroso. People's Daily. 2011-11-21.
41 XI J P. The governance of China. Beijing: Foreign Languages Press. 2014: 282.

An all-round, wide-ranged and multi-level cooperation pattern has been formed, a new path for developing China's relations with its traditional friendly partners has been opened up, an innovative practice for China-Europe relations has been adopted, and a new platform of South-South cooperation featuring characteristics of South-North cooperation has been set up. [42]

This is conducive to promoting the comprehensive and balanced development of China-EU relations. At the bilateral level, China and France have decided to open up a new era of a close and comprehensive strategic partnership; China and Germany have established a comprehensive strategic partnership; China and Britain have reached a consensus on creating a "Golden Age" of building a global comprehensive strategic partnership for the 21st century, to name just a few. Bilateral breakthroughs have further enhanced the level of China-EU cooperation and promoted greater development of China-EU comprehensive strategic partnership.

The BRICS countries are a model of cooperation between emerging and developing major countries. They have made important contributions to world economic stability and growth, improving global governance and promoting the democratization of international relations. China has always attached great importance to the cooperation between the BRICS countries, and actively promoted the cooperation between the BRICS countries from the original loose forum to the more institutionalized coordination mechanism, making the enhancement of their cooperation "a priority in our diplomatic agenda. We will always be a good friend, good brother and good partner of other BRICS countries."[43] With the spirit of openness, inclusiveness, cooperation and win-win result, the BRICS countries have endeavored to build a comprehensive and multi-level cooperative framework. Their cooperation areas have been expanding, their cooperation mechanism has been improving, and fruits of their cooperation have sprung out. The establishment of NDB and the launch of CRA will enable BRICS countries to have bigger say in international financial matters and help developing countries to resist international financial risks. On many major international and regional issues, the BRICS countries "rise and fall together, and share

---

42   Xi Jinping holds group meeting with CEEC leaders attending 4th Summit of China and CEEC. People's Daily. 2015-11-27.

43   XI J P. New departure, new vision and new impetus: remarks at the 6th BRICS Summit. People's Daily, 2014-07-17.

the same future, act as both a vitally interrelated interest community and a hand-in hand action community."[44] They have become an important force to promote the reform of the global governance system by upholding international fairness and justice, jointly speaking up, opening up a new path of the South-South cooperation, and strengthening the representativeness, equality and timeliness of the global governance system. Within the BRICS countries, China and India are both ancient civilizations of the world, facing historical development opportunities.

China and India should become closer partners for development who will jointly pursue their respective national rejuvenation; we should become cooperative partners for growth and jointly promote Asia's prosperity and revitalization; we should become global partners for strategic coordination and work for a more just and equitable international order.[45]

Brazil is the first developing country established strategic partnership with China and the first Latin American country established a comprehensive strategic partnership with China. China and Brazil regard each other as an important partner, and their bilateral relations continue to develop by entering into a more mature and stable new era. South Africa is China's largest trading partner in Africa. Africa's political ties with China are increasingly close, and our economic prospects are broad. China-South Africa relations are expected to become a new model of China-Africa strategic partnerships and a model of the solidarity and cooperation between major developing countries. The growth of the BRICS cooperation mechanism has been fluctuating, and the challenges lies in the BRICS countries are different. Only by enhancing mutual understanding and strengthening mutual learning can we promote the cooperation between China and the major developing countries to a higher level.

---

44 XI J P. Cement confidence and seek common development: speech at the 18th BRICS Summit Large-Scale Meeting. People's Daily. 2016-10-17.
45 XI J P. In joint pursuit of a dream of national rejuvenation: speech at the Indian Council of World Affairs. People's Daily. 2014-09-19.

Chapter 3

Implementing the Values of Friendship, Justice and Shared Interests

It is the core value orientation of Xi Jinping's diplomatic thought to adhere to the values of friendship, justice and shared interests in diplomatic work. It not only inherits and carries for ward the brilliant traditional Chinese moral and ethical standards of the Chinese culture, but also adds new meanings to mankind's treasure house of common values, gives expression to the inherent requirements of China's proposition to build a community of shared future for mankind and a new type of international relations. Implementing the values of friendship, justice and shared interests is of great significance for the practice of major-country diplomacy with Chinese characteristics. It will especially help China make new progress in its relations with the neighboring countries and the developing countries.

1. The proposition and connotations of the values of friendship, justice and shared interests

Since the 18th National Congress of the CPC, the new model of major-country relations with Chinese characteristics has entered into an active era with a pioneering and enterprising spirit. The values represented in China's diplomacy are related not only to its own international image, but also to world peace and development. General Secretary Xi Jinping conforms to the trends of the times of peace, development and win-win cooperation, puts forward that it is necessary to adhere to the values of friendship, justice and shared interests in diplomatic work, and makes a brilliant exposition on its connotations.

In March 2013, when visiting three African countries, President Xi Jinping put forward the concept of "the values of friendship, justice and shared interests" for the first time. He delivered a speech in Tanzania entitled "Trustworthy Friends and Sincere Partners Forever", in which he accurately summarized the substantive connotations of China's values of friendship, justice and shared interests in the new situations with four words: sincerity, real results, affinity and good faith. He pointed out that the essential characteristics of China-Africa relations are sincerity and friendship, mutual respect, equality and mutual benefit, and common development. XI also stressed that China should promote the common development of developing countries, help the poor countries as its capacity allows, and sometimes even value friendship and justice higher than interests or give up interests to friendship and justice. China must not be mercenary, squaring accounts in every detail.

In October 2013, at the conference on the diplomatic work on China's neighboring countries, General Secretary Xi Jinping further raised the values of friendship, justice and shared interests to the height of the basic policy guiding neighborhood diplomacy and developing countries diplomacy. He stressed, "We should seek common ground and find converging interests, stick to the sound values of justice and benefit, hold to the principles that we can act upon, cherish friendship and righteousness, and offer any assistance to developing countries that is within our means."[1]

In July 2014, when visiting the ROK, President Xi Jinping delivered a speech entitled Jointly Create a Beautiful Future of China-ROK Cooperation and Accomplish the Great Cause of Asia's Revitalization and Prosperity, in which he fully expounded the meaning and significance of practicing the sound values of justice and interests in international relations. Xi remarked,

> In dealing with international relations, we must abandon the outdated zero-sum mentality. We should not seek to gain more than others, to benefit ourselves at others' cost, not to mention the you-lose-I-win mentality, nor the winner-takes-all mentality. Only by taking both justice and benefit into consideration can we gain both; only by keeping the balance between justice and benefit can we win both.[2]

---

1   XI J P. The governance of China. Beijing: Foreign Languages Press. 2014: 299.
2   XI J P. Jointly create a beautiful future of China-ROK cooperation and accomplish the

At the Central Conference on Work Relating to Foreign Affairs held in November 2014, General Secretary Xi Jinping incorporated the concept of sound values of friendship, justice and shared interests into the concept of major-country diplomacy with Chinese characteristics. He advocated that, in the process of comprehensively promoting the external work under new conditions, "we should uphold justice and pursue shared interests. This means we should act in good faith, value friendship, and champion and uphold justice."[3] In the process of improving the diplomatic strategic planning, "we should truly uphold justice and pursue shared interests and do a good job in providing foreign aid, to actually advocate justice and share interests."[4]

In April 2015, during his visit to Pakistan, President Xi Jinping stressed, "We should advance our shared interests and achieve common development. The Chinese culture believes that to achieve success, one should let others succeed as well. China champions a right approach to principles and interests. We believe that to help Pakistan is to help ourselves."[5]

In September 2015, President Xi Jinping delivered a speech at the Development Summit Marking the 70th Anniversary of the United Nations and pointed out, "Facing the future, China will continue to uphold the principle of combining justice and interests and giving priority to justice,"[6] advancing the cause of global development. In the speech at the General Debate of the 70th Session of the UN General Assembly, President Xi Jinping restated, "Big countries should treat small countries as equals, and take a right approach to justice and interests by putting justice before interests."[7]

On November 21, 2016, when visiting Peru, President Xi Jinping delivered a speech entitled Set Sail in the Same Boat and Create a Beautiful Future for China-Latin American Relations, in which he re-emphasized the necessity

---

great cause of Asia's revitalization and prosperity: speech at Seoul National University of the Republic of Korea. People's Daily. 2014-07-05.
3   The central conference on work relating to foreign affairs was held in Beijing. People's Daily. 2014-11-30.
4   The central conference on work relating to foreign affairs was held in Beijing. People's Daily. 2014-11-30.
5   XI J P. Building a China-Pakistan community of shared destiny to pursue closer win-win cooperation: speech at the Parliament of Pakistan. People's Daily. 2010-04-25.
6   Speeches by Xi Jinping at the Series of Summits Marking the 70th Anniversary of the United Nations. Beijing: People's Publishing House. 2015: 5.
7   Ibid., 16.

of upholding justice and pursue shared interests by wishing that China-Latin American friendship last long like the evergreen pine trees. He said,

> China will adhere to the path of common development, continue to pursue a mutually beneficial and win-win result, actively implement the values of friendship, justice and shared interests, share our own development experience and opportunities with the rest of the world, and welcome all countries in the world to" hitch "China's development to achieve common development. China will continue to stand together with the vast number of developing countries and firmly support the increase of the representation and say of developing countries in the global governance system.[8]

In January 2017, President Xi Jinping reaffirmed at the United Nations Office in Geneva, "China will continue to uphold the value of justice and friendship and pursue shared interests, and boost pragmatic cooperation with other developing countries to achieve common development."[9]

With General Secretary Xi Jinping's repeated incisive explanations of the values of friendship, justice and shared interests with extensive quotes, the connotations and practice of the values are gradually substantiated and improved, becoming a banner of China's diplomacy in the new era. They enrich the value system of Xi Jinping's diplomatic thought, and provide theoretical guidance for major country diplomacy with Chinese characteristics. The so-called "values of friendship, justice and shared interests" mean to measure our own behavior with moral, justice, faith, friendship and other benchmarks in international relations. They do not mean that we cannot pursue interests, but that we pursue common interests that benefit all people. They do not mean that we cannot safeguard our national interests, but that in defending our national core interests and the bottom line we organically combine our own interests and other countries' interests to achieve the good result of benefiting both. In the exchanges with developing countries, the connotations of the values of friendship, justice and shared interests are more profound, which means that, with the sense of belonging and the sense of responsibility of a major developing country, China should take friendship and justice as its priority, patiently listen to the aspirations of the

---

8   XI J P. Set sail in the same boat and create a beautiful future for China-Latin American Relations: speech at the Peruvian Congress. People's Daily. 2016-11-23.

9   XI J P. Work together to build a community of shared future for mankind: speech at the United Nations Office at Geneva. People's Daily. 2017-01-20.

developing countries, take their interests and needs seriously and lend them a helping hand within its means, instead of bullying them or imposing its own interests on them and even on the common interests of all mankind.

> Justice reflects one of the ideas we hold as Communists in a socialist country. It is not a good phenomenon that some people in this world are living a very good life while some others are suffering from a very bad one. True happiness is common happiness for everyone to enjoy. We hope that the whole world will develop jointly, especially that the developing countries will accelerate their development. To have interests means to abide by the principle of mutual benefit and win-win result, to achieve a win-win result instead of the I-win-you-lose result.[10]

To uphold the values of friendship, justice and shared interests, in politics, we must uphold the principles of fairness and equality, abide by the basic principles of international relations, and oppose hegemonism. In economy, we must persist in mutual benefit and common development, and should especially consider more of the interests of those neighboring and developing countries who have been on long friendly terms with China and who are still confronted by the arduous task of their own development. We must not harm them to benefit ourselves, or shift our troubles onto them.

2. The inheritance and innovation in implementing the values of friendship, justice and shared interests

To implement the values of friendship, justice and shared interests is to inherit the moral essence of the Chinese traditional culture, the socialist values of justice and interests and the fine tradition of the New China's diplomacy since 1919, to conform to the trends of the times and the development trends of both China and global international relation sunder new historical background, and to innovate the code of conduct in international relations and the concept of South-South cooperation.

The issue of justice and interests constitutes the core of Chinese traditional culture. During the Spring and Autumn Period and the Warring States Period, various schools including Confucianism, Mohism and Legalists,

---

10 WANG Y. Upholding the values of friendship, justice and shared interests and actively playing the role of a responsible major country: profoundly understanding Comrade Xi Jinping's important speech on diplomacy. People's Daily. 2013-09-10.

had discussed the relationship between justice and interests, and formed a rich theory on the issue. For example, Confucius observed, "the mind of the superior man is conversant with righteousness; the mind of the mean man is conversant with gain", and that "the superior man values justice." Mozi, however, proposed that "justice is an interest" and clarified the unity of "justice" and "interests." Mencius advocated, "life is what I love, justice is also what I love. If I cannot keep the two both, I will let life go and choose justice." And there were still more. With the Confucian doctrine becoming a mainstream of traditional Chinese culture, such ideas as valuing justice over interests, the priority to justice over interests and obtaining interests in a proper way, have become the consistent moral standards and behavioral norms of the Chinese nation over thousands of years. They have crystalized as the dominant Chinese values in the course of historical accumulation, which not only have had a significant impact on Chinese people's lives, but also have shaped the magnificent bearing that makes China a big, accommodating country since the ancient times like a great river in its downstream. General Secretary Xi Jinping's thought on diplomatic work of upholding friendship, justice and shared interests applies traditional Chinese views on justice and interests to the practice of international relations in the 21ˢᵗ century, forming a new concept of major-country diplomacy with Chinese cultural heritage.

The thought of implementing the sound values of friendship, Justice and shared interests embodies the inherent requirements of socialism with Chinese characteristics, and the reference to and absorption of the socialist concept of justice and interests. The socialist concept of justice and interests is a scientific unity of justice and interests. In the relationship between morality and material gains, the socialist concept of justice and interests affirms that the material interests are the foundation of morality, and that the pursuit for legitimate material interests is reasonable. And meanwhile, it also emphasizes the role of moral regulations on material interests. In the relationship between public interest and self-interest, the socialist concept of justice and interests places public interest in the first place, while fully respecting the legitimate self-interests. As Mao Zedong said, "the public and the private are a unity of opposites. The public and the private cannot be sharply demarcated from each other. Therefore, we have always advocated taking both public and private interests into account.[11] The socialist concept of justice and interests emphasize the unity of justice and interests, and advocate the guidance of justice on interests, the acquirement of interests through justice, and the reflection on justice at the sight of interests, so that the two sides are engaged in both fair competition and mutual cooperation, that both economic benefits and social benefits are achieved, and that acts forsaking good for the sake of gold are opposed. General Secretary Xi Jinping's thought on diplomatic work of upholding friendship, justice and shared in interests, applying the essence of socialist concept of justice and interests into the international relations of the 21st century, and elucidates the relationship between international morals and national interests, enriching and supplementing the connotations of international relations ethics.

After the founding of the New China in 1949, it has always adhered to the establishment of friendly relations and cooperation with all countries in the world on the basis of the Five Principles of Peaceful Coexistence, and fully carried forward the spirit of internationalism in the exchanges with the countries of Asia, Africa and Latin America through establishing a fine tradition of emphasizing justice for the formation of the sound values of justice and interests. It is precisely under the guidance of the Five Principles of Peaceful Coexistence that China cannot only defy the arbitrary interference and pressure by super powers, but can adopt a position of understanding and consultation on the issue of border demarcation with medium neighbors for a fair and reasonable solution. From the early 1950s on, when its own economy was in very difficult situations, China began to provide all kinds of possible aid within its means to the vast number of newly independent nations in Asia, Africa and Latin America and supported them to achieve political independence, to maintain their overall national interests of economic development and livelihood improvement. In 1961, China announced the Eight Principles for Economic Aid and Technical Assistance to Other Countries, the core content of which featured equality, mutual benefit and with no strings attached, and establishing the basic principle of China's foreign aid. "By the end of 2009, China had provided a total of 256.29 billion CNY in aid to foreign countries, including 106.2 billion CNY in grants, 76.54 billion CNY

---

11 MAO Z D. Collected works of Mao Zedong: Vol. 8. Beijing: People's Publishing House. 1999: 134.

in interest-free loans and 73.55 billion CNY in concessional loans."[12] China's selflessness has laid a solid foundation for long-term friendly cooperation with developing countries, and has accumulated experience for implementing the values of friendship, justice and shared interests.

The important thought of General Secretary Xi Jinping on implementing the values of friendship, justice and shared interests is a major innovation of international relations and the South-South cooperation model in new situations. The sound values of justice and shared interests amend and surpass the gainful realist concepts of diplomacy, and demand China in its foreign exchanges never to follow the colonists' or the mercenary capitalists' example of raking in all possible pillage and profits, nor to seek to realize their own interests. They guide China to jointly pursue common development, progress and prosperity with all countries in the world instead. The sound values of justice and shared interests are contrary to the wrong values of justice and interests. In today's world, there still exist the narrow mindsets of international relations, such as zero-sum mentality, egoism and egocentrism. Such wrong values of justice and interests still keep resulting in or worsening crises and conflicts, leading to frequent frustrations in the cause of world peace and development. China thinks that "Humankind is now more capable than ever of making strides towards the goal of peaceful development. China proposes that all countries work together to turn pressure into impetus, turn crisis into the opportunity, and replace confrontation with cooperation and exclusive gain with mutual benefit."[13]

The sound values of justice and shared interests break the either this-or-that mode of thinking, overcome the empty talks of narrow egoism and hypocrisy, and insist on the equal stress on and the unity of justice and interests with forging a new concept of international relations with considerations for both morality and interests and providing value navigation for building a community of shared future for mankind. The correct treatment of the relationship between justice and interests demands that countries respect each other's core interests and major concerns in their relations, and emphasizes that they promote the common development of all countries in seeking their own development and that they organically integrate their own interests with

---

12   The State Council Information Office of the People's Republic of China. China's foreign aid. People's Daily. 2011-01-22.
13   XI J P. Speech at a Ceremony Marking the 95th Anniversary of the Founding of the Communist Party of China. Beijing: People's Publishing House. 2016: 20.

other countries' interests." With growing interaction among countries, problems are inevitable. What is important is that countries should resolve differences through dialogue, consultation and peaceful negotiation in the broader interest of a sound growth of their relations."[14] Implementing the sound values of justice and shared interests requires a dialectical approach to the relationship between morality and interests so as to achieve the unity of the two. China has always adhered to an independent foreign policy of peaceful development, and never wished to dominate, expand, or seek sphere of influence. China has always advocated a political solution to conflicts and disputes between nations. Meanwhile, peaceful development is not a unilateral act of China, nor is it a unilateral restrain on China. Only when all countries follow the path of peaceful development can they live together in peace. Anything that requires China to abandon its core interests on the excuse of its peaceful development, or interferes in China's internal affairs and issues to threaten China's survival, or challenges the bottom line of China is out of the question. General Secretary Xi Jinping solemnly pointed out,

> China's development will not be at t h e expense of the interests of other countries. Similarly, China's legitimate rights and interests are not to be violated. Exchanging China's sovereignty, dignity and unity for interests will both damage China's core and major interests and lead to distortions in values of justice and interests.[15]

In implementing the sound values of justice and shared interests, we especially consider more of the interests of those neighboring and developing countries who have been on long friendly terms with China and who are still confronted by the arduous task of their own development. This reflects China's exploration of a new model of South-South cooperation, highlighting China's international obligations. Equality and mutual benefit are well-established norms of international cooperation. But to the least developed countries with specific needs, China often gives unilateral preferential treatment besides the principle of reciprocity, or advocates valuing friendship and justice over interests. Sometimes China even gives up interests for friendship and justice if necessary in the cooperation with them. "In cooperation with developing countries, China will stick to the correct idea of righteousness and benefit and refuse' I-win-you-lose or I-much-you-little'

14   XI J P. The governance of China. Beijing: Foreign Languages Press. 2014: 331.
15   Xi Jinping gives joint interview to media from BRICS countries. People's Daily. 2013-03-20.

mentality and will care for interests of the other side in some specific projects."[16] As a major developing country, in the South-South cooperation, China's "selfless concepts and practice won the respect, trust and supports from the wide range of developing countries."[17] Years ago, internationalism was the supreme guiding principle for the relationship between China and developing countries. With China's national strategic focus shifted to economic construction, the ideological overtones of internationalism faded in its diplomatic practice. And now internationalism is guiding the relationship between China and developing countries in the context of the new era, and is endowed with new meanings. From this point of view, the practice of the sound values of justice and interests reflects the spirit of altruism in the relationship between China and developing countries. It strongly supports the economic development and social progress of developing countries, and promotes world peace and stability. These are conducive to shaping China's international image as are sponsible major country, and to refuting the theories of "China threat" "neo-colonialism" and other erroneous views.

3. Strengthening the solidarity and cooperation with developing countries

Strengthening the unity and cooperation with developing countries is the basic principle of China's foreign policy. China has consistently adhered to and stressed its identity as a developing country, and has regarded the vast majority of developing countries as fellows along the path of peaceful development. The relationship between China and the developing countries has gone through a severe test of various situations such as the Cold War between the United States and the Soviet Union and the great changes in the international landscape after the Cold War, and has been pushing forward steadily. The development of economy is the first task faced by China and developing countries. China supports the economic construction of developing countries and understands the position of developing countries in opposing interferences from the Western countries in the internal affairs relating to their political security. It is working with developing countries to

---

16   XI J P. Help each other in crisis and jointly create a new era for the development of the China-Mongolia relations. People's Daily. 2014-08-23.

17   WANG Y. Upholding the values of friendship, justice and shared interests and actively playing the role of a responsible major country: profoundly understanding Comrade Xi Jinping's important speech on diplomacy. People's Daily. 2013-09-10.

build a new international order and to promote the evolution of the world towards multipolarization. "The friendship based on interests will break when no more profits come in; the friendship built on power and influence will tumble when power and influence are forfeited; only the friendship that grows out of genuineness and sincerity will last long."[18] Since the 18th CPC National Congress, under the leadership of the CPC Central Committee with Comrade Xi Jinping as the core, China's diplomacy has implemented the sound values of friendship, justice and shared interests, insisted on sincere friendship and equal treatment with developing countries. It has further reinforced bilateral high-level exchanges, enhanced dialogues and consultation on different levels, and made new progress in the relations between China and other developing countries, comprehensively promoting China's friendly and cooperative relations with Africa, Latin America, the Arab countries and the Pacific Islands.

China-Africa relations are on a "fast-track" of all-round development. "China and Africa have always been a community of shared destiny. The similar historical experiences, common development tasks as well as shared strategic interests have bound the two sides together."[19] In 2013, during President Xi Jinping's visit to Africa, he put forward the guiding principles on China-Africa relations of "faithfulness, honesty, affinity and sincerity", and pointed out the following principles: in treating African friends, China will remain faithful; in conducting cooperation with Africa, China will value real results; in strengthening friendship with Africa, China will seek to cultivate kinship-like qualities in the relationship; in addressing problems in China-Africa cooperation, China will be sincere. His words clarify the connotations and the significance of the sound values of friendship, justice and shared interests. In 2011, during the Ebola outbreak, China firmly stood in the forefront in the global cooperation and helped Liberia, Guinea, Sierra Leone and other West African countries to fight the epidemic, offered a lot of personnel and material support and fulfilling China's commitment to the construction of a China-Africa community of shared destiny.

---

18 XI J P. Jointly create a beautiful future of China-ROK cooperation and accomplish the great cause of Asia's revitalization and prosperity: speech at Seoul National University of the Republic of Korea. People's Daily. 2014-07-05.
19 XI J P. The governance of China. Beijing: Foreign Languages Press. 2014: 305.

China and Africa both shoulder the mission of developing our respective countries and improving the livelihood of two peoples. Africa enjoys abundant natural and human resources and has reached the stage of taking off in industrialization. China, after reform and opening-up of over 30 years, now has the technology, equipment, professional and skilled personnel and capital needed to help Africa realize sustainable self-development. In particular, China has the strong political commitment to supporting Africa in achieving development and prosperity. China and Africa share mutual needs and complementarities and face a rare historic opportunity in pursuing development through cooperation.[20]

At the end of 2015, at the Johannesburg Summit of the Forum on China-Africa Cooperation, President Xi Jinping announced that the new type of China-Africa strategic partnership would be upgraded to a comprehensive strategic and cooperative partnership. To forge this partnership, China and Africa should strengthen the following "five major pillars": commitment to political equality and mutual trust, commitment to win-win economic cooperation, mutual enrichment of cultural exchanges, commitment to mutual assistance in security, and commitment to solidarity and coordination in international affairs. At this summit, President Xi Jinping put forward ten China-Africa cooperation plans of 60 billion USD of grant in the next three years, raising the concept and practice of China-Africa cooperation to a new height at the same time. The ten cooperation includes industry, agriculture, infrastructure, finance, green development, trade and investment facilitation, poverty reduction, public health, cultural and people-to-people communication, and peace and security. At present, China-Africa relations are in the best period in history. Looking into the future, China and Africa are always good friends, good partners and good brothers. As President Xi Jinping said, "no matter how the international situation changes, China will firmly adhere to the friendly foreign policy to Africa, remain reliable friends and sincere partners of African countries, and strive to make greater contributions to Africa's cause of peace and development."[21]

---

20   XI J P. Open a new era of China-Africa win-win cooperation and common development: speech at the opening ceremony of the Johannesburg Summit of the Forum on China-Africa cooperation. People's Daily. 2015-12-05.
21   The development of China-Africa relations only in the progress tense and never in the perfect tense. People's Daily. 2013-03-29.

Although China is far apart from Latin America and the Caribbean countries, they have a long history of friendly relations. The rapid escalation of China-Latin American cooperation is another outstanding embodiment of the implementation of the sound values of friendship, justice and shared interests.

> China and Latin America share the same approach to development. We have found increasingly more common language whether in respective nation building and governance or in international affairs. Facts have proven, and will continue to show, that the growth of China-Latin America relations is an open and inclusive process featuring win-win cooperation. It not only serves the common interests of the two sides, but also contributes to peace, stability and prosperity in the region and the world at large.[22]

In July 2014, President Xi Jinping visited Brazil, Argentina, Venezuela, Cuba and some other Latin American countries. In the meeting with Latin American leaders, he delivered a keynote speech and announced that China and the Latin American countries would "establish the China-Latin America comprehensive cooperative partnership of equality, mutual benefit and common development, and build up a Five-in-One new pattern of China-Latin America relations: sincerely trust each other in politics, cooperate with each other for a win-win result in economy and trade, learn from each other in people to-people and cultural exchanges, closely cooperate with each other in international affairs, and promote each other in overall cooperation and bilateral relations"[23], so as to forge a hand-in-hand community of common destiny for China and Latin America. These new ideas and new initiatives pointed out the direction and established the goal of efforts for China-Latin American relations. President Xi Jinping creatively proposed the "1+3+6" cooperation framework between China and Latin America. "1" means "one plan" referred to the establishment of the China-Latin American Countries and Caribbean States Cooperation Plan (2015-2019). "3" means "three engines" referred to promoting the comprehensive development of China-Latin America practical cooperation with trade, investment and financial cooperation as the impetus. "6" means "six fields" referred to boosting China-Latin America industry connection with

---

22 President Xi Jinping gives a joint written interview to the media of Trinidad and Tobago, Costa Rica and Mexico. People's Daily. 2013-06-01.

23 XI J P. Striving to build a hand-in-hand community of common destiny: keynote speech at the China-Latin America and the Caribbean Summit. People's Daily. 2014-07-19.

energy and resources, infrastructure construction, agriculture, manufacturing, scientific and technological innovation, and information technologies as cooperation priorities. This cooperation framework aims to achieve inclusive growth and sustainable development, strives to promote China-Latin America trade 10 scale up to 500 billion USD and the investment stock to Latin America up to 250 billion USD within ten years. During Xi's visit, China and Latin American countries jointly announced the establishment of the Forum of China and Community of Latin American and Caribbean States (CELAC), promoting China-Latin American cooperation from the unitary type of mainly bilateral cooperation to the compound type of bilateral and multilateral cooperation. This marks the global coverage of the regional multilateral cooperation framework initiated by China and intended for developing countries, and improves the layout of China's diplomatic relations with developing countries.

At the beginning of 2015, The First Ministerial Meeting of the CELAC released three outcome documents, namely the Beijing Declaration of the First Ministerial Meeting of the CELAC-China Forum, China-Latin American and Caribbean Countries Cooperation Plan (2015-2019), and the Institutional Arrangements and Operating Rules of CELAC-China Forum, pushing the China-Latin American cooperation from the concept level to a new stage of effective realization. In November 2016, China's Policy Paper on Latin America and the Caribbean was issued, comprehensively expounded China's new policies, new ideas, and new initiatives in its foreign policy on Latin America in the new era to promote their cooperation in various fields to achieve greater development." Currently, China-Latin American relations are in a new historical period. With the establishment of CELAC as a symbol, the overall cooperation between China and Latin America successfully set sail. China and Latin America have joined hands to promote our comprehensive cooperative partnership featuring equality and mutual benefit and common development to build a community of common destiny, and opened up broad prospects for our cooperation in various fields."[24]

The Arab countries are located at the joint of the western end of the Belt and Road Initiative. They arc not only the hub area for the realization

---

24   President Xi Jinping sends congratulatory letter to the 10th China-LAC Business Summit. People's Daily. 2016-10-15.

of the interconnection between Asia, Africa and Europe, but also natural partners for China to implement the sound values of friendship, justice and shared interests and to develop its traditional friendship and cooperation with other developing countries. "At present, China-Arab relations are standing at the new starting point of inheriting the past and ushering in the future, and the development of the China-Arab relations is mainly characterized by peace and cooperation, openness and inclusiveness, mutual learning, mutual benefits and win-win results."[25] The ancient Silk Road has long linked China to the Arab countries. China and the Arab countries are good friends, good brothers and good partners with mutual respect, mutual recognition and mutual trust.

China cherishes its relations with the Arab countries and has always promoted the development of China-Arab relations from a strategic and long-term perspective. To the Arab friends, we insist on "Four Unwavering Initiatives." First, China unwaveringly sticks to the position of supporting the Middle East peace process and safeguarding the legitimate rights and interests of the Arab countries. Second, China unwaveringly sticks to the direction of advancing a political settlement and promoting peace and stability in the Middle East. Third, China unwaveringly sticks to the idea of supporting Arab countries to independently explore the road of development and helping their development. Fourth, China unwaveringly sticks to the values of promoting the dialogue between civilizations and advocating a new order of civilizations. We are willing to go hand in hand with the Arab countries on their respective ways to achieve national rejuvenation.[26]

In June 2014, President Xi Jinping proposed at the Ministerial Conference of China-Arab States Cooperation Forum held in Beijing that China and the Arab countries jointly construct the Belt and Road, forge a community of common interests and a community of common destiny, and build a "1+2+3" cooperation pattern with energy cooperation as the main axis, infrastructure construction and trade and investment facilitation as the two wings, and the three high-tech areas of nuclear energy, aerospace satellite and new energy as breakthroughs. By 2016, China and the Arab countries have setup the mechanism of strategic and political dialogue, and

---

25 Xi Jinping sends congratulatory letter to years of China-Arab friendship. People's Daily. 2014-09-11.

26 Xi Jinping meets with heads of Arab delegations attending the sixth ministerial conference of China-Arab States Cooperation Forum. People's Daily. 2014-06-06.

China has entered into strategic partnership with eight Arab countries and signed agreements with six Arab countries on jointly developing the Belt and Road Initiative. President Xi Jinping made four points on China-Arab relations and stressed that "China and the Arab countries need to pursue independent paths of development, to defend regional peace, to carry out mutually beneficial cooperation, and to advocate cultural diversity."[27] In the Middle East, hot spots are so many and contradiction are so complicated that political solution is the only realistic way to resolve the differences and disputes. China is willing to promote dialogue in a constructive manner to solve regional hot issues and uphold justice. Guided by the sound values of justice and interests, "China will continue to unswervingly support the Middle East and Arab states in preserving their ethnic and cultural traditions, and oppose all forms of discrimination and prejudice against specific ethnic group and religion."[28] China, together with the Arab countries, will make unremitting efforts in inheriting and passing down traditional cultures and maintaining the diversity of civilizations.

Pacific Island countries are an important part of developing countries and an important member of the Asia-Pacific region. They are uniquely important geographically, economically and politically. Despite the great distance, the Chinese people and the people of the Pacific Island countries enjoy a long history of friendship and have natural sense of amity. In the 1970s, China established diplomatic relations with eight Pacific Island countries, and since then the friendly cooperative relations between the two sides have developed rapidly." For decades, mutual respect, mutual support, sincere friendship, mutually beneficial cooperation and common development have always been the key words of China's relations with the Pacific Island countries."[29] In November 2014, during his visit to Fiji, President Xi Jinping held a group meeting with leaders of the Pacific Island countries, such as Fiji, Micronesia, Samoa, Papua New Guinea and Vanuatu. All the participants agreed to establish a strategic partnership featuring mutual respect and common development. China sincerely welcomes the Pacific Island countries to board the train of China's development for a fast

---

27 XI J P. Let China-Arab friendship surge forward like the Nile. People's Daily. 2016-01-20.

28 XI J P. Work together for a bright future of China-Arab relations: speech at the Arab League Headquarters. People's Daily. 2016-01-22.

29 XI J P. Be a lasting true friend of the Pacific Island countries. People's Daily. 2014-11-22.

ride, to share each other's experiences and achievements in development, to strengthen exchanges and cooperation in various fields, to deepen their friendship and to work together in the journey of realizing their respective dreams.

4. Fulfilling the obligations of a responsible major country

As an old Chinese saying goes, "a state should not regard material gains as its interests, but take justice as its interests." Since the 18th CPC National Congress, General Secretary Xi Jinping has fully interpreted and attached great importance to the sound values of friendship, justice and shared interests, which have become the compass that guiding China's diplomatic practice, pushing China to participate in international affairs more actively and better playing the role of a responsible major country.

The world today is in an adjustment period featuring great change and great development. On the one hand, with the constant accumulation of material wealth and ever-changing scientific and technological progress, human civilization has developed to an unprecedented level in history; on the other hand, global economic growth is weak, development gap is increasingly widening, regional conflicts occur frequently, such global challenges as terrorism, refugee crisis and major infectious diseases rise one after another and the world is faced with growing numbers of uncertainties. Standing at the crossroads of history, as a responsible major country, China cannot and will not stay aloof." Being a big country means shouldering greater responsibilities for regional and world peace and development, as opposed to seeking greater monopoly over regional and world affairs."[30] In whichever era, if big countries live in harmony, the world will have peace and stability; if big countries become enemies, the world will suffer turmoil and conflicts. Living in a world where the interests of all countries are intertwined and the fate of all human beings are inseparable, the major countries should take the overall situation of human peace and development as the most important issue, work together and help one other by providing a shelter for the world rather than going their own way, managing alone, or even confronting one another.

30　XI J P. Towards a community of common destiny and a new future for Asia: keynote speech at the Boao Forum for Asia Annual Conference 2015. People's Daily. 2015-03-29.

China has always been a responsible major country. Being aware of the preciousness of peace and the value of development, China has regarded promoting world peace and development as its sacred duty, and has strived to do its utmost in assuming reasonable international responsibilities. In the 1990s, China articulated that it would b e a responsible big country, which reflects China's strong sense of responsibility and sacred sense of mission. As China's strength grows, its ability to assume the obligations of a major country significantly improves, and its will to fulfill the obligations of a responsible major country becomes increasingly strong.

The Chinese people are patriotic. Yet we are also a people with a global vision and an international perspective. As its strength grows, China will assume more international responsibilities and obligations within the scope of its capabilities and make greater contribution to the noble cause of world peace and development.[31]

On the one hand, the role of China as a responsible major country is embodied by shouldering responsibilities for China itself, doing their own things well, safeguarding China's domestic security and stability, and prosperity and development, protecting the well-being of the Chinese People. China is the world's most populous developing country, maintaining and developing its economy and improving its people's livelihood are the primary responsibilities of the Chinese government. Every achievement that China has made is also a step of progress for the whole world. This responsibility is taken both for China itself, and for the world at large. The people are the foundation of a country, and a country's national interests are inseparable from those of its people. Being a responsible major country, China adheres to the people-oriented concept of diplomacy, focuses on the domestic reality needs, and takes the initiative to serve the improvement of people's livelihood. Besides, it builds overseas livelihood projects and effectively safeguards the legitimate rights and interests of Chinese citizens and enterprises.

---

31 President Xi Jinping gives joint interview to media from BRICS countries. People's Daily. 2013-03-20.

On the other hand, a responsible major country is responsible for the world. President Xi Jinping elaborated on China's approach to the status of a responsible major country in international relations from the following three levels: first, China will more actively and effectively maintain world peace, propose a common, comprehensive, cooperative and sustainable concept of security, and commit itself to peacefully solve disputes through negotiations. It firmly maintains the UN-centered post-war international order, and actively participates in UN peacekeeping operations and regional security dialogues and cooperation. Second, China will more actively and effectively participate in international affairs, stay committed to promoting the improvement of international governance system, enhance and enlarge the representation and voice of developing countries in international affairs, propose more Chinese programs, contribute more China's wisdom, and provide more public goods for the international community. Third, China will more actively and effectively promote common development, uphold the values of friendship, justice and shared interests, balancing the two sides and giving priority to justice, promote North-South dialogue and South-South cooperation, and in particular, help developing countries achieve independent and sustainable development.[32]

Foreign aid is an important way for China to fulfill its obligations as a responsible major country. Since the founding of the New China in 1949, while devoted to its own development, China has insisted on providing aids for economically difficult developing countries within its means, taking on the corresponding international obligations, and achieving fruitful results, creating a model of foreign aid with Chinese characteristics. By 2015, China has provided nearly 400 billion-CNY to assist 166 countries and international organizations, and dispatched more than 600,000 aid workers, of which more than 700 Chinese citizens have devoted their precious lives to the development of other countries.[33] On the Central Conference on Work Relating to Foreign Affairs in 2014, General Secretary Xi Jinping emphasized that we should truly uphold justice and pursue shared interests and do a good job in providing foreign aid, to actually advocate justice and

---

32   Xi Jinping gives joint interview with media from four Latin American and Caribbean countries. People's Daily. 2014-06-15.

33   Speeches by Xi Jinping at the Series of Summits Marking the 70th Anniversary of the United Nations. Beijing: People's Publishing House. 2014: 5.

share interests,[34] which profoundly reveals the importance of foreign aid under the guidance of the sound values of friendship, justice and shared interests.

In September 2015, on the occasion of the 70th anniversary of the founding of the UN, President Xi Jinping delivered a speech entitled Towards Win-Win Partnership for Sustainable Development at the United Nations Sustainable Development Summit and a speech entitled Promoting Women's All-round Development and Building a Better World for All at the Global Leader s' Meeting on Gender Equality and Women's Empowerment. In the speeches, he announced the five important initiatives on the China's foreign aid: first, China will establish an assistance fund for South-South cooperation with an initial pledge of 2 billion USD in support of developing countries' implementation of the post-2015 development agenda. Second, China will exempt the debt of the outstanding intergovernmental interest free loans due at the end of 2015 owed by the relevant Least Developed Countries (LDCs), landlocked developing countries and small island developing countries. Meanwhile, China will continue to increase investment in the LDCs, and aims to increase its total to 12 billion USD by 2030. Third, in the coming five years, China will provide other developing countries with "six 100 projects" including 100 poverty reduction projects, 100 agricultural cooperation projects, 100 hospitals and clinics, 100 schools and vocational training centers, 100 ecological protection and climate change projects, and 100 trade promotion and foreign aid projects. Fourth, China will set up a South-South Institute for Cooperation and Development to provide academic education and training places to train talents came from other developing countries. In the next five years, China will provide 120,000 training places and 150,000 scholarships to the students and scholars of other developing countries and will cultivate 500,000 professional and technical personnel for other developing countries. Fifth, in the coming five years, China will help other developing countries by building 100 "health projects for women and children," send teams of medical experts to provide services, and implement 100 "happy campus projects" to finance the schooling of poor girls and raise the girls' school enrollment rate. China will also host 30,000 women from developing countries for training programs in China

---

34 The central conference on work relating to foreign affairs was held in Beijing. People's Daily. 2014-11-30.

and provide 100,000 professional and technical skills training opportunities for women in local communities of other developing countries.[35]

The above-mentioned aid measures fully reflect General Secretary Xi Jinping's diplomatic thought of building a community of shared future for mankind and implementing the sound values of friendship, justice and shared interests, and declare to the world that China is actively taking on the responsibilities of a major country and that it is determined and willing to work with other developing countries to achieve common development. These aid measures have received wide acclaim from the international community. China's foreign aid policy has distinctive characteristics of the times, and is in line with its own national conditions and the recipient countries' development needs. As the largest developing country, China is still faced with the arduous long-term task of development, which determines that China's foreign aid belongs to the category of South-South cooperation and therefore, is a type of mutual help between developing countries. The above-mentioned aid measures show that China intends to help recipient countries to improve their capacity for self-development in providing assistance to them, and that China has made great efforts to cultivate local talents and technical forces for recipient countries to help them in their infrastructure construction. The measures are mainly developed for their social and livelihood projects, benefiting the community-level organizations, laying the foundation for development, and promoting the recipient countries to gradually embark oneself reliance and independent development. China will never attach any political conditions when providing assistance, and will never use assistance as a means of interfering in the internal affairs of other countries and seeking political privileges, but respects the rights of the recipient countries to choose their own path and mode of development instead. China believes that the recipient countries can find the development path suited to their own national conditions. The practice of the China's foreign aid is a typical embodiment of the sound values of justice and interests. While helping other developing countries to improve their people's livelihood and promote their social progress, China improves its international image of a responsible major country and strengthens its international influence.

---

35 For the details of these five initiatives, please refer to Speeches by Xi Jinping at the Series of Summits Marking the 70th Anniversary of the United Nations. Beijing: People's Publishing House. 2015: 5-6, 12; Xi Jinping delivers speech at high-level roundtable on the South-South cooperation. People's Daily. 2015-09-28.

General Secretary Xi Jinping's thought and practice of the values of friendship, justice and shared interests have established a moral foundation for exploring the path of major-country diplomacy with Chinese characteristics, deepened the relationship between China and other developing countries, and enriched the traditional concept of South-South cooperation by contributing Chinese wisdom to the theory and practice of international relations. Under the guidance of the sound values of justice and interests, China actively fulfills its obligations as a responsible major country for the benefit of both the Chinese people and the peoples of other countries, and strives to create a new situation of diplomatic work in the new era.

Chapter 4

Leading the Reform of the Global Governance System

Since the 18th CPC National Congress, based on the strategic needs of realizing the "Two Centenary Goals" and the Chinese Dream of the great rejuvenation of the Chinese nation, General Secretary Xi Jinping has scientifically studied the profound changes in the current international system and international landscape, and made a series of important speeches on global governance and the reform of the global governance system, which have clarified China's views on global governance, and developed the theoretical system of major-country diplomacy with Chinese characteristics. As he pointed out,

> China will actively participate in developing the international governance system, contribute Chinese wisdom for improving global governance, and work with the peoples of all countries in pushing the international order and global governance system towards a more just and equitable direction.[1]

---

1 XI J P. Speech at a Ceremony Marking the 95th Anniversary of the Founding of the Communist Party of China. Beijing: People's Publishing House. 2016: 20.

1. The proposition of the reform of the global governance system

Global governance is the inevitable outcome of globalization. After the end of the Cold War, the wave of globalization swept the world. With economy as its center, the wave gradually spread to politics, society, culture and other fields with reflecting the increasing interdependence between countries. However, the global problems that endanger the future of all mankind are also spreading at the same time. Facing up with increasingly serious global problems, sovereign states' coping capacity is clearly inadequate. As a new concept of international cooperation, the idea of global governance came into being in the 1990s. The so-called "global governance" refers to the system, norms, mechanisms and activities that manage international affairs established by the international relations actors such as sovereign states, international organizations and non-governmental organizations with the purpose of solving the global problems and enhancing the common interests of all mankind. The concept of global governance provides a broader paradigm of international cooperation for solving common problems faced by mankind and a new perspective for understanding international relations. Its values are universally recognized by the international community. Since the beginning of the new century, with the acceleration of globalization and the continuous deepening of interdependence between all countries, the international community's demand for global governance has been further enhanced. At the same time, the international political and economic situation sees continuous unrest and repeated failures in the attempts of global governance to solve it, though the practice of global governance has extended from armament control, regional hot spots, development assistance and climate change to international anti-terrorism, international public health, international financial order and other issues. After the 2008 international financial crisis, the call for reforming and improving the global governance system has become increasingly urgent, providing a strategic opportunity for the rising China to participate in global governance. The 18th CPC National Congress in 2012 proposed for the first time the guidelines for China's foreign strategy "to increase exchanges and cooperation with other countries and promote reform in global governance,"[2] which indicated that China

---

2   HU J T. Firmly march on the path of socialism with Chinese characteristics and strive to complete the building of a moderately prosperous society in all respects: report to the 18th National Congress of the Communist Party of China. People's Daily. 2011-11-18.

would actively seek the leadership of global governance and contribute its wisdom and strength to the global governance system. This is an important part in major-country diplomacy with Chinese characteristics and is one of the China's historic commitments to be a responsible major country.

In October 2015, at the twenty-seventh group study session of the Politburo of the 18th CPC Central Committee, General Secretary Xi Jinping clearly put forward that, the core of China's ideas of global governance was mutual consultation, efforts and sharing. Mutual consultation means to do brainstorming in the process of global governance in emphasizing the common participation of all countries in the world, advocating the democratization of international relations. The reform of the global governance system requires that the fate of the world must be grasped by the people of all countries. Global affairs have to be handled in mutual consultation by the governments and the peoples of all countries. We should fully respect each country's rights to independently choose its own path of development and to participate in global governance. We should endeavor to make the global governance system more even and more reflective of the will and interests of most countries. This is the democratic principle of dealing with international affairs, which the international community should abide by. In particular, the representation and voice of emerging market countries and developing countries should be increased, so that their equality in rights and opportunities in international economic cooperation can be promoted. Mutual efforts mean that all countries pull well together and do their best in the process of global governance, giving full play to their respective advantages. The reform of the global governance system requires that all countries strengthen their awareness of global cooperation, expand the areas of global cooperation, and improve the forms of global cooperation. Major countries should play a leading role in global governance and make greater contributions. Especially, "China and the US share broad interests in this respect and should work together to improve the global governance system. This will not only leverage our respective strengths to enhance cooperation, but also enable our two countries to jointly respond to major challenges facing mankind."[3] Mutual sharing means that all countries share the fruits of global governance, so that these fruits can more equitably benefit all countries and all peoples in the world. The prosperity and stability of the world cannot be established on

---

3　Stick to the right direction of building a new model of major-country relation between China and the US: promote the peaceful and stable development of the Asia-Pacific region and the world. People's Daily. 2015-09-23.

the basis of a number of countries being increasingly affluent while the others being poor and backward for long. Only when all countries achieve common development can the world witness better development. The acts of harming others to benefit oneself or shifting one's own burden of crises onto others arc neither moral nor durable. In short, the concept of global governance featuring mutual consultation, efforts and sharing means that global governance has to be implemented by all countries and all peoples of the world through consultation, that a more comprehensive global governance system has to be built by countries and all peoples around the world, and that the fruits of global governance has to be shared by all countries and all peoples. This concept of global governance voices China's idea on the reform of the global governance system and its framework for promoting the reform, and contributes Chinese wisdom to the reform, showing that China is not only an active advocate, but also the leader of the reform of the global governance system.

In September 2016, on the G20 Hangzhou Summit, with the theme of "Towards an Innovative, Invigorated, Interconnected and Inclusive World Economy," achieved results of ground breaking, guiding and institutional significance, which provided a new idea for the world to get out of the global economic predicament. During the summit, President Xi Jinping systematically expounded for the first time a comprehensive vision of global economic governance which is based on equality, oriented toward openness, driven by cooperation and aimed at shared interests. He also pointed out the priority areas and tasks of cooperation, depicted a roadmap for improving the global economic governance system, and left a deep Chinese imprint in the history of the G20. President Xi Jinping said,

> At this stage, global economic governance should focus on four aspects: jointly ensure equitable and efficient global financial governance and uphold the overall stability of the world economy; jointly foster open and transparent global trade and investment governance to cement the multilateral trading regime and unleash the potential of global cooperation in economy, trade and investment; jointly establish green and low-carbon global energy governance to promote global green development cooperation; jointly facilitate an inclusive and interconnected global development governance to implement the UN 2030 Agenda for Sustainable Development and jointly advance the well-being of mankind.[4]

---

4   XI J P. A new starting point for China's development, a new blueprint for global growth: keynote speech at the opening ceremony of the B 20 Summit. People's Daily. 2016-09-04.

Global economic governance is the foundation and core of global governance. Reforming global economic governance is the key to the problems of injustice and irrationality in global governance. Its main task is to increase the power of developing countries, especially the power of the emerging major developing countries, under the existing governance framework, and constantly update a new mechanism that can reflect the changes in the balance of international powers. The G20 Leaders' Communique Hangzhou Summit drafted and led by China reflects China's visions of innovation-driven development, coordinated development, green development, open development and sharing development proposed by President Xi Jinping. It embodies China's solutions to the fundamental problems confronting the world economic growth, and integrates China's propositions which advocate building a community of shared future for mankind and improving the global economic governance. These concepts, programs and ideas have become an international consensus, receiving wide support from all par ties in the G20. The concepts, programs and ideas not only give better play to the G20's role as the banner in global economic governance, but also lead China to participate in global economic governance on higher, wider and deeper dimensions.

Facing the rise of conservatism and isolationism in the world in recent years, the international community is looking forward to strengthening global governance. In January 2017, President Xi Jinping attended the World Economic Forum in Davos and delivered a key note speech, in which he profoundly explained the objective inevitability of economic globalization, analyzed the problems with current world economic growth, governance and development models, and proposed to create a dynamic growth model, an open and win-win cooperation model, a fair and reasonable governance model, and an equitable and inclusive development model, contributing the Chinese vision to the world economic development. President Xi pointed out, "People with petty shrewdness attend to the trivial matters, while people with vision attend to the governance of institutions. There is a growing call from the international community for reforming the global economic governance system, which is a pressing task for us. Only when it adapts to new dynamics in the international economic architecture can the global governance system sustain global growth."[5] Emerging markets and developing countries have

______

5   XI J P. Jointly shoulder responsibility of our times, promote global growth: keynote

already contributed 80% of the growth to the global economy. The global economic landscape has changed profoundly. However, the global governance system has not embraced those new changes and is therefore inadequate in terms of representation and inclusiveness. Therefore, it is essential to give more representation and say to emerging markets and developing countries. President Xi Jinping's proposal on global governance can help us to eliminate the negative impacts of the anti-globalist counterflow and boost the international community's confidence in the reform of the global governance system, which in turn establishes China's positive image of leading global governance.

2. China's opportunities in leading the reform of the global governance system

"The global governance system reform is inseparable from the guidance of the right concept."[6] China's initiative for the reform of the global governance system is to promote the international order and global governance towards a more just and rational direction which is more conducive to developing countries. China will take the following position: "What kind of international order and governance system best suits the world, and best suits the people of all countries? This is something that should be decided by all countries through consultation, and not by a single country or small minority of countries."[7] The reform of the global governance system is not a matter of a single country or of a small number of countries, but requires the joint efforts of the entire international community, especially those of the major countries. At the same time, China does not seek to revolutionize the current global governance system, "such reform is not about dismantling the existing system and creating a new one tore place it. Rather, it aims to improve the global governance systemin an innovative way. We in China have a saying, ' when all means are exhausted, changes are necessary; once changes are made, things will be improved.' Either for a country or the entire world, keeping pace with the times is necessary in order to maintain its vigor."[8]

---

speech at the opening session of the World Economic Forum Annual Meeting 2017. People's Daily. 2017-01-18.

6   Promote the global governance system to be more just and reasonable and create favorable conditions for China's development and world peace. People's Daily. 2015-10-14.

7   XI J P. Speech at a Ceremony Marking the 95th Anniversary of the Founding of the Communist Party of China. Beijing: People's Publishing House. 2016: 20.

8   Stick to the right direction of building a new model of major-country relations between China and the United States: promote the peaceful and stable development of the Asia-Pacific Region and the world. People's Daily. 2015-09-23.

The current global governance system emerged from the post World War II power structure in many aspects and is the sum of the relevant institutions, principles, procedures and modes of operation that are coordinated and managed in all areas of international relations under the auspices of the Western developed countries headed by the US. Specifically, the global governance system includes the international security system with the UN collective security system as the core, the international monetary and financial system with the IMF and the World Bank as the core, the international trade system with the WTO as the core, and so on. The global governance system in all fields and at all levels not only establishes the legitimacy foundation for global governance and develops codes of conduct, but also provides a basic framework for the operation of global governance. However, the current global governance system is increasingly unable to meet the increasing demands for global governance, and cannot deal with the spread of global problems effectively. The plight of "governance failure" calls for the reform and innovation of the global governance system, and creates conditions for China to participate in the reform of the global governance system. At the global level, in recent years, the reforms of the UN and the IMF and the rise of the G20 are all implementations of institutional reforms for more effective global governance. At the regional level, the needs of governance are relatively concentrated so it is easier to form a consensus on interests. The institutional transformation and construction of the regional organizations such as the EU, AU and ASEAN, have promoted the effectiveness of global governance in the regional scope. Their transformation and construction expand the denotations of such regional system and help to achieve governance in a greater scope. The global governance theory itself is inadequate, the global governance model is still in the exploratory stage, and the concept of global governance can only be effectively popularized through institutional change. China is aware that,

Strengthening global governance and promoting the reform of the global governance system has become their resistible trend. It is not only a matter of dealing with global challenges, but also a matter of setting rules for the international order and the international system; it is not only related to the competition of the commanding heights of development, but also related to each country's status and role in the long-term institutional arrangements of international order and the international system. [9]

Since the beginning of the 21st century, the trend of multipolarization of the world has continued to advance. The collective rise of the emerging countries has especially given China the dynamics to participate in the reform of the global governance system. After the Cold War, the United States failed to build a stable US-dominated unipolar world. All kinds of forces in the world have been developing constantly, and their influence on international affairs has been on the rise to different degrees, which greatly promotes the development of multi polarization. In addition to the US, the EU, Russia, Japan, China and other forces, the emerging regional developing countries, with their fast growing strength, are also playing an important role. They are a new driving force of multipolarization of the world. The change in the balance of power between countries is the basic driving force behind the reform of the global governance system. Since the beginning of the 21st century, the developing countries, represented by the BRICS countries, have experienced rapid economic growth and are displaying a collectively rising trend. The 2008 financial crisis accelerated the power shift process, resulting in the change of the structural center of world economy and the corresponding change in the power structure of global governance. Against this background, new governance systems began to spring up, and the lagging governance systems were adjusted. Some of the new governance systems reflect the attempts of emerging countries to seek overall advantages, such as the BRICS' mechanism; some are re-allocations of voice in the existing global governance, such as the reforms of IMF and the World Bank; some are alternatives to the original governance system, such as the G20 which replaced the G 8 and became the primary forum for international economic coordination; some are supplements to the existing governance system, such as the implementation of the AIIB and the NDB. Reform and adjustment at different levels of the

---

9   Promote the global governance system to be more just and reasonable and create favorable conditions for China's development and world peace. People's Daily, 2015-10-14.

global governance system, as well as the increase of the representation and voice of developing countries, have become the irresistible trend. The absolute dominance of developed countries in global governance gradually gave way to joint decision-making by both developed countries and emerging countries. Emerging countries not only share the responsibilities of developed countries as partners, but also express their interest demands in an aggregative way and play a role in the reform and remodeling of the global governance system.

China's participation in global governance has gone through a tortuous process from the edge to the center. In the new century, in the rise and fall of the balance of power between major countries, the rise of China is the most eye-catching. With the improvement of its national strength and the progress of its diplomatic ideas, China gradually changes from a participant in global governance to a maker of international rules and a provider of international public goods. Its discourse power in global governance has greatly improved, becoming the key force in promoting the evolution of the international order. The expectations of international community for China have generally increased. They hope that China will make a positive contribution to the reform of the global governance system. After Xi Jinping became the Chinese President in March 2013, he talked about global governance in an interview on the eve of his first visit to a foreign country. He said, "the global economic governance system must reflect the profound changes in the global economic landscape. The representation and voice of emerging markets and developing countries should be increased."[10] At the Boao Forum for Asia Annual Conference in April 2013, President Xi Jinping stressed," we should steadily advance there form of the international economic and financial systems, improve global governance mechanisms and provide support to sound and stable global economic growth."[11] In September 2015, President Xi Jinping pointed out again in an interview on the eve of his visit to the United States," as the global landscape evolves and major transnational and global challenges facing mankind increase, it is necessary to adjust and reform the global governance system and mechanism."[12] In October 2015, the Politburo of the CPC Central Committee

---

10   President Xi Jinping gives joint interview to media from BRICS countries. People's Daily. 2013-03-20.

11   XI J P. The governance of China. Beijing: Foreign Languages Press. 2014: 330.

12   Stick to the right direction of building a new model of major-country relations between China and the United States: promote the peaceful and suitable development of the Asia-Pacific Region and the World. People's Daily. 2015-09-23.

held a group study session on global governance structure and the global governance system, which proposed "to promote the reform of the unjust and improper arrangements in the global governance system."[13] At the G20 Hangzhou Summit in 2016, China fully explained its concept of global economic governance for the first time. On September 27, 2016, the Politburo of the CPC Central Committee held group study session on global governance and stressed that,

> To strengthen global governance and promote global governance system reform is the irresistible trend. We must seize the opportunity and ride the wave to make the international order more reasonable and just, to better safeguard the common interests of China and the vast majority of other developing countries, to create more favorable external conditions for the realization of the "Two Centenary Goals" and the Chinese Dream of the great rejuvenation of the Chinese nation, and to make greater contributions to the noble cause of the human peace and development.[14]

3. Strengthening China's contribution to the reform of the global governance system

At present, as a participant, builder and leader of global governance, China not only contributes ideas of global governance to the world, but also promotes the healthy, equitable and orderly development of global governance with practical and vigorous pace. In the process of participating in the reform of the global governance system, China insists on speaking out for developing countries and strengthening solidarity and cooperation with them. It has always stressed that it will strive for more rights for the developing countries, especially in global economic governance. China clearly stated that, it is important to "increase the representation and voice of the developing countries and give all countries equal right to participate in international rule-making."[15]

---

13   Promote the global governance system to be more just and reasonable and create favorable conditions for China's development and world peace. People's Daily. 2015-10-14.

14   Strengthen cooperation to pursue reforms to the global governance system and advance the noble cause of peace and development for mankind. People's Daily. 2016-09-29.

15   Speeches by Xi Jinping at the Series of Summits Marking the 70th Anniversary of the United Nations. Beijing: People's Publishing House. 2015: 3.

In the field of political security, China will "firmly uphold the international system with the UN as the core, the basic norms governing international relations embodied in the purposes and principles of the UN Charter, the authority and stature of the UN, and its core role in international affairs". [16] The international order after World War II is hard-won and the norms of international relations represented by the UN Charter are precious. Respect sovereignty and oppose interference; maintain peace and oppose aggression; adhere to dialogue and oppose violence; support equality and oppose power. These ideas are timeless and unfading and consistently considered as the principles of the China's diplomacy. The confrontations and injustices in today's world are not because the purposes and principles of the UN Charter arc outdated, but precisely because these purposes and principles have not been effectively fulfilled. To this end, the UN must carry forward institutional reforms to adapt to the changes in international balance of power and meet the needs of global governance. China has always attached great importance to and supported the reform of the UN. It has always argued that the reform of the UN should help realize the principles of the UN Charter, fulfill the heavy tasks given to the UN by the times, reflect the principle of regional balance, and enhance the status and role of developing countries in the UN. China is a permanent member of the UN Security Council featuring the largest developing country. On the matter of reform, China must both uphold the position of developing countries and assume the responsibilities as a major country. In the face of serious differences in the reform programs put forward by different countries, China believes that the reform of the UN should be gradual and progressive, and it is necessary to take a cautious approach to the major issues on which there remain differences and not to set a time limit or force a decision. The reform of the UN Security Council is closely related to China's vested status as a big political power. China's proposition is compatible with the values of democracy, equality and cooperation advocated by the UN, with a view to increasing the representation and voice of developing countries. At present, in the permanent member of the UN Security Council, China sends the most peacekeepers and ranks second-place in paying its share towards peacekeeping operations. China has contributed to the political

---

16 XI J P. Work together to build a community of shared future for mankind: speech at the United Nations Office at Geneva. People's Daily. 2017-01-20.

solutions to such hot spot issues as the reconstruction of Afghanistan, the Syrian civil war and the Iran's nuclear crisis, and played an important role in safeguarding world peace and security. In September 2015, President Xi Jinping attended a Series of Summits Marking the 70th Anniversary of the UN, during which he put forward a series of pragmatic cooperation measures, including establishing a 10-year, 1 billion USD China-UN peace and development fund to support the UN's work, joining the new UN Peacekeeping Capability Readiness System, taking the lead in setting up a permanent peacekeeping police squad and building a peacekeeping stand by force of 8,000 troops, and soon. These measures show that China has actively taken practical action to reform and improve the capacity of the UN to implement global governance.

In the economic field, China's measures to promote global governance system reform are the most effective. After the 2008 international financial crisis, speeding up the reform of the global international economic organizations with the IMF and the WTO as the core became the objective requirements to achieve global economic stability and sustainable and balanced growth. China has become an important engine of world economic growth. China's position and role in world economy is not only reflected in China's economic strength and competitiveness, but also embodied by China's participation in global economic governance and decision-making power. Promoting the reform of global international economic organizations is the objective need of the global governance system reform and of the inevitable requirement of China's economic strength. China supports the IMF's leading position in the restructuring of the international financial system, advocates the establishment of a fair, just, inclusive and orderly international financial system.

> Continue to strengthen the international financial market supervision so that the financial system really relies on, serves and promotes the real economic development. Build a stable and anti-risk international monetary system, conduct reform on the Special Drawing Rights (SDR) currency basket, strengthen the connections among international and regional financial cooperation mechanisms, and build a financial risk firewall.[17]

---

17   XI J P. The governance of China. Beijing: Foreign Languages Press. 2014: 338.

With the IMF approving the Chinese Yuan to join the SDR currency basket and the share reform program taking effect, the Chinese Yuan has become one of the world's five largest reserve currencies, China's share in the IMF has risen to the third place, and China's status in the international monetary and financial power structure has been further improved. At the G20 Hangzhou Summit in September 2016, China set "improving global economic and financial governance, enhancing the representation and voice of emerging markets and developing countries, and raising the ability to resist risks in the world economy" as one of the main topics, promoted the establishment of a more stable and resilient international financial architecture with all other parties, and enhanced their confidence to improve global financial governance. The reform of the WTO is imperative because of the long delay in the Doha round of trade negotiations. China's role as the world's largest exporter and second largest importer is equally important in the reform process. China has always maintained the status of the WTO as the main channel in global trade and investment, and supported promoting the development of the WTO decision-making mechanism toward a more effective and transparent direction. Although innovations in the current global trade governance arc more reflected in the negotiation and implementation of various regional trade agreements, in the long run, regional trade agreements cannot replace the WTO, and global trade liberalization featuring profit maximization is the common pursuit of all countries in the world. The multilateral trading system centers around the WTO, and its vitality lies in its inclusiveness and non-discrimination. When we participate in regional free trade cooperation, we must adhere to the principle of openness, inclusiveness and transparency, so that the cooperation is both beneficial to the participants and reflective of our support to the multilateral trading system and rules, to avoid fragmentation of the global trade governance system.

In order to strengthen the reform of the global economic governance system, China positions the G20 as the main platform for global economic governance, and has taken positive measures to construct the G20 so that it will "truly help stabilize the world economy, drive global growth and enhance global economic governance."[18] The G20 Leaders' Summit started at

---

18 XI J P. Promoting innovative development achieving interconnected growth: remarks at Session one of the Ninth G20 Summit. People's Daily. 2014-11-16.

the critical juncture of the 2008 international financial crisis. In November 2008, the first G20 Leaders' Summit was held in Washington, DC. Then it began to move from the edge of global economic governance to the center and was gradually established as the main platform for dealing with the financial crisis. Member countries of the G20 reached many consensuses on the reform of the existing international financial institutions and rules, and joined hands to adopt a series of economic stimulus plans. Since then, the G20 has replaced the G8 as the main forum for world economic cooperation. Its role orientation has also changed from a simple response to the financial crisis to a major platform for promoting global economic cooperation. After 2011, the Leaders' Summit-Ministerial Conference-Working Group Meeting institutional structure came in to being, which marked the beginning of the equal participation of developing countries represented by emerging countries in global economic governance. The G20 Hangzhou Summit in September 2016 is the highest, largest and most influential international summit that China has hosted in recent years. At this summit, China "for the first time gave a comprehensive interpretation of China's concept of global economic governance, for the first time treated innovation as the core result, for the first time put the development issues in the prominent position of the global macroeconomic policy coordination, for the first time formed a global multilateral investment rules framework, for the first time released a Presidential statement on the issue of climate change, and for the first time included green finance in the G20 agenda, leaving a profound imprint of China on the history of the G20."[19] The G20 Hangzhou Summit has enriched the consensus of the international community on global economic governance and fully demonstrated China's wisdom and contribution of participation in global economic governance while promoting the transformation and development of the G20. In the area of development, China has been actively involved in the UN development agenda. In September 2015, President Xi Jinping pointed out at the UN Sustainable Development Summit that "I would like to pledge China's solemn commitment to take implementation of the post-2015 development agenda as its bounden duty and work together with other countries

---

19   Strengthen cooperation to pursue reforms to the global governance system and advance the noble cause of peace and development for mankind. People's Daily. 2016-09-29.

for continued progress in global development."[20] At the same time, China announced a series of major initiatives including the establishment of an assistance fund for South-South Cooperation and the China South-South Climate Cooperation Fund, to promote international development cooperation and help developing countries to achieve sustainable development. In the UN development system, China has changed from a former aid recipient to an emerging major donor country. It has the responsibility and ability to play a leading role in the process of implementing sustainable development goals, and realize its blueprint for global governance system reform. In September 2016, China was the first to release China's National Plan on Implementation of the 2030 Agenda for Sustainable Development, providing experience and reference for other countries, especially developing countries, to promote their implementation work. It is precisely because of China's efforts that the G20 Hangzhou summit adopted the G20 Action Plan on the 2030 Agenda for Sustainable Development. This is the first time that the development agenda has been listed as the core issue for the G20. In order to strengthen global efforts to tackle the issue of climate change, China has also played the leading role of a responsible major country. Speaking at the 2015 Climate Change Conference in Paris, President Xi Jinping systematically put forward China's proposal to deal with global climate change and called on all countries to reach a comprehensive, balanced, ambitious and binding agreement on climate change, contributing China's strength to the promotion of global climate governance.

In the area of emerging global issues, China is proactive and actively seeks to tackle the global challenges of governance, proposing that "China needs to play a bigger role in making rules for new areas including the Internet, the polar regions, deep sea and outer space, and will extend greater support to cooperation mechanisms and projects on educational exchange, dialogue among civilizations and ecological conservation."[21] The ever-changing technology and the rapid development of globalization have brought more and more complicated and complex global problems to the human society. Seeing from the height of building a community of shared future for mankind, China advocates forward-looking explorations of emerging

---

20 Speeches by Xi Jinping at the Series of Summits Marking the 70th Anniversary of the United Nations. Beijing: People's Publishing House. 2015: 6.
21 Strengthen cooperation to pursue reforms to the global governance system and advance the noble cause of peace and development for mankind. People's Daily. 2016-09-29.

areas on the basis of the common welfare of mankind. Since 2014, China has launched and held the World Internet Conference every year to build a platform for China and the world to be interoperable and for the Internet to be shared and commonly governed. It is a successful attempt in the governance of emerging fields. President Xi Jinping put forward in the Chinese program the following four principles of global Internet governance: respecting the cyber sovereignty of different countries, maintaining peace and security, advancing opening-up and cooperation, and building sound order. To lay the foundation for the international community to establish a multilateral, democratic and transparent global Internet governance system, he further put forward five proposals, namely, speeding up the building of global cyber infrastructure, building an online platform for cultural exchanges and sharing, promoting the innovation-driven development of a cyber-economy, maintaining cyber security, and building an Internet governance system.[22]

4. China's innovation to promote the reform of the global governance system

General Secretary Xi Jinping's important thought on the global governance system is not only a scientific theoretical system, but also a strategic action guide. In the face of the new situation, new problems and new demands of the development of the world today, it is difficult for the existing global governance system to effectively deal with them. It is riddled with a great number of loopholes, fuzzy space and blank areas, therefore, it is necessary to promote there form of the existing system, and strengthen the construction of a new model of governance system through institutional innovation. To this end, General Secretary Xi Jinping pointed out,

> We will play a more active role in international affairs, commit ourselves to improving international governance system, and make vigorous efforts to increase the representation and voice of developing countries in international affairs. We will offer more Chinese solutions, contribute China's wisdom and provide the international community with more public goods.[23]

22   XI J P. Speech at the opening ceremony of the Second World Internet Conference. People's Daily. 2015-12-17.
23   President Xi's joint interview with media from four Latin American and Caribbean countries. People's Daily. 2014-07-15.

The international financial system dominated by the Western countries has long been unable to give China sufficient representation and voice. In order to promote its participation in global financial governance and strengthen its decision-making power in the international financial system, with its rising financial strength, China has made great efforts in recent years to promote innovation in the fields of international economic and financial and surrounding regional cooperation, and strengthened the construction of new rules and regulations, including implementing the Belt and Road Initiative, advocating the establishment of the AIIB and the Silk Road Fund, and participating in the establishment of the NDB and other new international financial mechanisms, giving a strong impetus to the global governance system towards a more just and reasonable direction. The Belt and Road Initiative is China's "active exploration of a new model of international cooperation and global governance,"[24] and China's strategic concept of building a community of shared future for mankind. It does not focus on a single entity or organization, but is an unprecedented systematic project, designed to create an inclusive and open platform for cooperation and to create a new type of international cooperation model. Promoting the strategic docking and complementary advantages on the basis of existing cooperation is not only in line with the needs of China's further opening up and development, but also meets the development needs of the participating countries. It is a major innovation in China's national development strategy and foreign policy. In this project, financial innovation is the most typical. The establishment of the AIIB and the launch of Silk Road Fund are both innovative highlights in implementing the Belt and Road Initiative. These events have not only injected a new impetus into China's economic growth, but also provided new ideas and new programs for global governance, and opened up a new road of international cooperation for the rest of the world. They are China's significant contribution to the reform of the global governance system.

The AIIB is a multilateral development financial institution whose preparation and construction is led by China and whose nature is inter-governmental. It is a milestone in the China-promoted reform of the global governance system. In October 2013, when President Xi Jinping held talks with Indonesian President Susilo in Jakarta, he proposed an initiative to build the AIIB for the first time.

---

24   Vision and Actions on Jointly Building the Silk Road Economic Belt and 21st Century Maritime Silk Road. Beijing: People's Publishing House. 2015:3.

To promote the process of interconnection and economic integration in the region, China proposes to build the AIIB and is willing to provide financial support to the developing countries' infrastructure construction in the region, including the ASEAN countries. The AIIB will cooperate with and complement the existing multilateral development banks outside the region to jointly promote the sustained and stable development of the Asian economy.[25]

In October 2014, representatives from the first group of 22 Prospective Founding Members signed the Memorandum of Understanding on Establishing the Asian Infrastructure Investment Bank in Beijing, deciding to set up the AIIB. In June 2015, representatives from 50 Prospective Founding Members signed the Articles of Agreement of the Asian Infrastructure Investment Bank. In December 2015, seven other Prospective Founding Members left their signatures on the Agreement. In December 2015, the Agreement met the legal threshold for entry into force and the AIIB was officially founded. The number of Prospective Founding Members increased to 57, including 37 in Asia and 20 out of Asia, covering Asia, Oceania, Europe, Latin America and Africa, with broad international representation. On January 16, 2016, the AIIB officially opened. President Xi Jinping pointed out at the inauguration ceremony,

China has taken an active part in, contributed a constructive part and benefited from the international development system. The initiative to establish the AIIB is a constructive move. It will enable China to undertake more international obligations, promote improvement of the current international economic system and provide more international public goods. This is a move that will help bring mutual benefits and win-win outcomes to all sides.[26]

After the establishment of the AIIB, countries and regions around the world competed to join. As of May 2017, the total number of the AIIB members reached 77. The AIIB upholds open regionalism and seeks complement and common development with the existing multilateral development banks. China, as the initiator of the AIIB, will firmly support its

25 China, Indonesia lift ties to comprehensive strategic partnership. People's Daily. 2013-10-03.
26 XI J P. Address at the Asian Infrastructure Investment Bank Inauguration Ceremony. People's Daily. 2016-01-17.

operation and development. In addition to subscribing capital according to plan, China will contribute 50 million USD to the project preparation special fund to be established soon, to support the preparation for infrastructure development projects in less developed member states. The principles of openness, inclusiveness, negotiation, consensus of decision-making, non-intervention of internal affairs, and so on, in the process of its founding show that the AIIB is very different from the international financial institutions dominated by the Western countries. Its operation will make up for the funding gap in infrastructure construction in Asia, promote regional interconnection and economic integration, while improving the international development financing system, and guide the direction of the reform of the global financial governance system.

The Silk Road Fund is a special fund China has set up for implementing the Belt and Road Initiative and to develop the Eurasian continental economy. On November 1, 2011, General Secretary Xi Jinping presided over the eighth meeting of the Central Leading Group on Financial and Economic Affairs, which for the first time stated, "China will set up the Silk Road Fund with the aim of directly supporting the construction of the Belt and Road."[27] After this meeting, at the Dialogue on Strengthening Connectivity Partnership, China formally pledged to contribute 40 billion USD to set up the Silk Road Fund." The Silk Road Fund is open and can be set up according to region, industry or project type. Investors both in and out of Asia are welcome to participate actively."[28] In December 2014, the Silk Road Fund was incorporated in Beijing and was officially launched. As a medium and long-term development investment fund, the Silk Road Fund adheres to the concept of "opening-up and inclusiveness, mutual benefit and win-win result," provides investment and financing support for economic and trade cooperation as well as bilateral and multilateral interconnection in the Belt and Road Initiative, and promote the common development and common prosperity of both China and countries and regions along the Belt and Road routes.

---

27   Speed up the construction of the Silk Road Economic Belt and the 21st Century Maritime Silk Road. People's Daily. 2014-11-07.
28   XI J P. Connectivity leads to development and partners focus on cooperation: speech at the dialogue on strengthening connectivity partnership. People's Daily. 2014-11-09.

The NDB was the first multilateral financial institution to be established by emerging countries that had broken through regional confines. It was announced at the Sixth BRICS Summit in July 2014 and officially opened in July 2015. The NDB focuses on long-term development financing, while simplifies the mutual settlement and loan transactions among BRICS countries, reducing the reliance on the USD and the euro. At the same time, the establishment of the CRA is focused on financial stability, so as to solve the fund shortage of BRICS countries and other developing countries in infrastructure and other fields, and resist market volatility. The CRA is an important complement to the current global financial system, which manifests that the BRICS countries have become an important force in reforming global financial governance. For a long time, developing countries have been keeping voiceless in the marginal status in the international financial system. But they are often the fragile links in financial globalization and financial liberalization, vulnerable to erosion from financial crises. China wants to play an important role in the global financial governance system reform, it shall "well establish, maintain and develop the two mechanisms of the NDB and the CRA, to provide strong protection for the economic development of developing countries"[29], and enhance the role of developing countries in global financial governance.

In addition to guiding the innovation initiatives in the economic and financial sectors, General Secretary Xi Jinping also offered forward-looking views and propositions on China's capacity to participate in global governance. He stressed that China should actively explore the resonance of the philosophy of life and governance ideas in Chinese excellent culture and the current era to promote the innovation and development of the global governance concept and related capacity building and personnel training as well. More fair and reasonable requirements of global governance cannot be separated from the absorption of the outstanding achievements of mankind. The traditional Chinese culture is broad and profound, and it is the unique contribution of traditional Chinese wisdom to give play to the advantages of traditional Chinese culture and integrate it into the global governance concept. On the problems of the relatively weak capacity of the current global governance and the lack of global governance personnel, General Secretary

---

29   XI J P. Cement confidence and seek common development: speech at the 8th BRICS Summit. People's Daily. 2016-10-17.

Xi Jinping proposed that "we should strengthen capacity-building and strategic investment, strengthen the theoretical study of global governance, and attach great importance to the cultivation of global governance talents."[30] Taking China's own situation into consideration, General Secretary Xi Jinping stressed that capacity building could be conducted from four aspects: rule-making capacity, agenda-setting capacity, publicity capacity and coordination capacity.[31] For talents who are to implement China's participation in global governance, General Secretary Xi Jinping proposed the quality requirements from six aspects: "being familiar with the Party's and national policies, understanding China's national conditions, having a global perspective, being fluent in foreign languages, being proficient in international rules, and being proficient in international negotiations."[32]

General Secretary Xi Jinping's thought on the reform of the global governance system not only has distinctive Chinese characteristics, but also fully reflects the responsibility of China and the rest of the world to deal with global issues and safeguard common interests of mankind. At present, China is playing a leading role in the reform of the global governance system. With its national strength further enhanced, China will take a more enterprising attitude and more effective measures to promote the global governance system in a more just and reasonable direction, making greater contributions to the realization of the "Two Centenary Goals" and Chinese Dream of the great rejuvenation of the Chinese nation and to the world's peace and development.

---

30   Promote the global governance system to be more just and reasonable and create favorable conditions for China's development and world peace. People's Daily. 2015-10-14.
31   Strengthen cooperation to pursue reformist to the global governance system and advance the noble cause of peace and development for mankind. People's Daily. 2016-09-29.
32   Ibid.

Chapter 5

Advancing the Belt and Road Construction

The Belt and Road Initiative are the solution proposed by China for common prosperity and development of the world, focusing on the common aspirations of the peoples of the world for peace and development. It is a valuable inspiration drawn from the China's ancient Silk Road and full of Eastern wisdom. As a Chinese systematic idea for building a community of shared future and forging a new model of international relations, the Belt and Road Initiative is an important part of Xi Jinping's diplomatic thought, which fully embodies the great resource fulness and great wisdom of the new generation of Chinese leadership who has accurately grasped the profound changes in the world situation and opened up a new broader space for development.

1. The proposition of the Belt and Road Initiative

The Silk Road originated in ancient China. It was an artery of trade and cultural exchange went across the East and the West and connecting Europe with Asia. For thousands of years, it carried great missions of promoting the progress of human civilization, accelerated the communication between the Eastern and the Western civilizations, and facilitated exchanges, cooperation and development fruits sharing among the countries along the Belt and Road. After the beginning of the 21st century, on the one hand, global issues have become increasingly prominent, forcing countries to help each other to alleviate multiple challenges; on the other hand, the new technological revolution has enhanced the development and flourish of transportation and Internet information dissemination technologies, turning the whole world into a highly cohesive "village". In the face of the stagnant global economic situation and the complex international political situation, the mission of inheriting and carrying forward the spirit of the Silk Road becomes more important. The Belt and Road Initiative is a major strategic decision made by the leadership of the CPC Central Committee with Comrade Xi Jinping as the core, and an important step in the implementation of a new round of opening-up. As General Secretary Xi Jinping said: "the Belt and Road Initiative will be equipping the roe of China with two wings. Sound implementation of the Belt and Road Initiative makes the roc fly higher and farther."[1]

On September 7, 2013, during his visit to Kazakhstan, President Xi Jinping delivered an important speech entitled Promote People-to-People Friendship and Create a Better Future, in which he demonstrated his grand vision and friendship, and proposed to build the Silk Road Economic Belt for the first time.

> To forge closer economic ties, deepen cooperation and expand development space in the Eurasia region, we should take an innovative approach and jointly build the Silk Road Economic Belt. This will be a great undertaking for the people of all countries a long the routes. To turn this vision in to reality, we may start in specific areas and connect them over time to cover the whole region. We need to set up policy consultation, improve road connections, promote unimpeded trade, enhance monetary circulation and increase understanding between our peoples.[2]

On October 3, 2013, when President Xi Jinping visited Indonesia, he delivered a speech entitled Jointly Build a Community of Common Destiny for China and ASEAN Members, and expounded the bright prospect of extending the Silk Road Initiative to the sea." Southeast Asia has since ancient times been an important hub along the ancient Maritime Silk Road. China will strengthen maritime cooperation with the ASEAN countries, and the China-ASEAN Maritime Cooperation Fund set up by the Chinese government should be used to develop maritime partnership in a joint effort to build the Maritime Silk Road of the 21st century."[3] By now, the Belt and Road Initiative takes its basic shape.

---

1 The Publicity Department of the CPC Central Committee. General Secretary Xi Jinping's important remarks (2016 Edition). Beijing: Xuexi Publishing House. 2016: 266.
2 XI J P. The governance of China. Beijing: Foreign Languages Press. 2014: 289.
3 Ibid. 293.

In November 2013, the Decision of the CPC Central Committee on Major Issues Concerning Comprehensively Deepening Reform was adopted by the Third Plenary Session of the 18th CPC Central Committee. The Decision spelt out China's commitment to "work hard to build the Belt and Road Initiative, so as to form a new pattern of all round opening-up."[4] The Belt and Road Initiative was officially upgraded to the top-level design of China's diplomatic relations. In December 2013, on the Central Economic Work Conference, General Secretary Xi Jinping pointed out in his speech, "we will implement the construction of the Silk Road Economic Belt, press on the strategic planning, and strengthen the construction of infrastructure connectivity. We will construct the 21st century Maritime Silk Road, strengthen the construction of maritime connectivity, and intensify the tie of common interests."[5] The Belt and Road Initiative enters into the stage of strategic planning.

On May 21, 2014, President Xi Jinping delivered a keynote speech entitled New Asian Security Concept for New Progress in Security Cooperation at the Fourth Summit of the Conference on Interaction and Confidence Building Measures in Asia (CICA), in which he deeply explained the guiding ideas and value orientation of the Belt and Road Initiative. He said,

> China will work with other countries to speed up the construction of a new economic belt along the Silk Road and a 21st century Maritime Silk Road, and hopes that the AIIB can be launched at a nearly date. China will be more involved in the regional cooperation process, and play its part to ensure that development and security in Asia facilitate each other and are mutually reinforcing.[6]

On June 5, 2014, President Xi Jinping delivered a speech entitled Promoting Silk Road Spirit and Deepening China-Arab Cooperation at the opening ceremony of the Sixth Ministerial Conference of the China-Arab States Cooperation Forum. He stated, "China and the Arab states enjoy mutual understanding and friendship because of the Silk Road, and are natural cooperative partners in jointly building the Belt and Road. The two sides should adhere to the principle of discussion, co-construction and sharing, and build a community of common interests and a community of

---

4   Decision of the CPC Central Committee on Major Issues Concerning Comprehensively Deepening Reform. People's Daily. 2013-11-16.

5   Central Economic Work Conference held in Beijing. People's Daily. 2013-12-14.

6   XI J P. The governance of China. Beijing: Foreign Languages Press. 2014: 358.

common destiny."[7] On the basis of reviewing the profound friendship between the Arab countries and China, he pointed out the present and future potential of the Belt and Road Initiative.

On September 18, 2011, President Xi Jinping delivered a speech entitled In Joint Pursuit of a Dream of National Rejuvenation at the Indian Council of World Affairs, in which he made it clear, "the Belt and Road Initiatives aimed at strengthening connectivity among countries along the traditional land and maritime Silk Roads, with a view to achieving common prosperity, complementarity in trade and closer people-to-people ties. China hopes that, propelled by the two' wings' of the Belt and Road Initiative, its economy will take off together with those of the South Asian countries."[8] In November of the same year, the eighth meeting of the Central Leading Group on Financial and Economic Affairs adopted the Plan of the Silk Road Economic Belt and the 21st century Maritime Silk Road, and required to work out the overall Belt and Road Initiative, and to determine the time tables and road maps for the coming years for the Belt and Road Initiative as soon as possible. In March 2015, the National Development and Reform Commission, the Ministry of Foreign Affairs and the Ministry of Commerce of the People's Republic of China jointly issued the Vision and Actions on Jointly Building Silk Road Economic Belt and 21st Century Maritime Silk Road, which was an indication that Belt and Road Initiative had entered the implementation phase from the initiation phase.

On March 28, 2015, President Xi Jinping, when attending the opening ceremony of the Boao Forum for Asia Annual Conference, reinterpreted the connotations of the Belt and Road Initiative. He stressed that the programs in the Belt and Road Initiative will be open and inclusive, not exclusive. They will be a real chorus comprising all countries along the road, not a solo for China itself. To develop the Belt and Road Initiative is not to replace existing mechanisms or initiatives for regional cooperation. Much to the contrary, we will build on the existing basis to help countries align their development strategies and form complementarity.[9]

On November 7, 2015, President Xi Jinping delivered an important speech at the National University of Singapore entitled Deepen Cooperative

---

7   XI J P. The governance of China. Beijing: Foreign Languages Press. 2014: 316.

8   XI J P. In joint pursuit of a dream of national rejuvenation: speech given at the Indian Council of World Affairs. People's Daily. 2014-09-19.

9   XI J P. Towards a community of common destiny and a new future for Asia: keynote speech at the Boao Forum for Asia Annual Conference 2015. People's Daily. 2015-03-29.

Partnership and Co-build Beautiful Homeland of Asia, stressing that the Belt and Road Initiative features development, cooperation and openness, and that China's primary partners and beneficiaries are in China's neighborhood. "Neighboring countries are welcomed to join the Belt and Road Initiative so as to jointly realize the outlook of peace, development and cooperation."[10]

On November 18, 2015, when President Xi Jinping attended the APEC CEO Summit, he pointed out:

> We adhere to open regionalism. We have signed cooperation agreements with many countries inside and outside the region, to achieve policy and development strategy docking, and to promote the orderly free flow of economic elements, efficient allocation of resources and the deep integration of markets. Through implementing the Belt and Road Initiative, we will go for even broader, deeper and more sophisticated cooperation at the regional level and jointly foster a regional framework of open, inclusive, balanced and mutually beneficial cooperation.[11]

On January 19, 2016, President Xi Jinping published a signed article titled Let China-Arab Friendship Surge Forward like the Nile on Egyptian newspaper al-Ahram, which described the goals of the Belt and Road Initiative as true common prosperity instead of the mere satisfaction of self-interests. He called on China and Egypt to jointly build the Belt and Road Initiative, link up their respective development strategies, deepen and expand cooperation in such areas as energy, trade and investment, infrastructure construction and high technology. He wrote, "China welcomes Egypt and other Arab countries to get on board the fast train of its development and hopes that our respective development and growth could be well aligned and mutually reinforcing."[12]

In March 2016, China released the 13th Five-Year Plan, which listed the Belt and Road Initiative as a special chapter.

On June 22, 2016, President Xi Jinping delivered a speech titled Jointly Compose a New and Splendid Chapter of the Silk Road during his visit to Uzbekistan. In the speech, he proposed to promote the Belt and Road

---

10 XI J P. Deepen cooperative partnership and co-build beautiful homeland of Asia: speech at the National University of Singapore. People's Daily. 2015-11-08.
11 XI J P. The Leading role of the Asia-Pacific in meeting global economic challenges: speech at the National University of Singapore. People's Daily. 2015-11-19.
12 XI J P. Let China-Arab friendship surge forward like the Nile. People's Daily. 2016-01-20.

Initiative towards a higher and broader space, and highlighted that they jointly forge such new concepts as "Green Silk Road" "Healthy Silk Road" "Intellectual Silk Road" and "Peaceful Silk Road,"[13] which fully demonstrated President Xi Jinping's grand vision of, firm belief in and good outlooks for the close cooperation between China and countries along the routes in areas including environmental protection, health care, personnel training and security work.

On August 17, 2016, the Symposium on the Belt and Road Initiative was held. General Secretary Xi Jinping noted: "The progress and results of the Belt and Road Initiative have been greater than expected."[14] Further, he raised eight requirements for the construction of the Belt and Road Initiative including unified thinking, coordination, financial innovation, cultural cooperation, security and so on.

On January 17, 2017, when President Xi Jinping delivered a speech at the Opening Session of the World Economic Forum Annual Meeting in Davos, he summed up the benefits the Belt and Road Initiative had brought to the world: over 100 countries and international organizations had given warm responses and support to the initiative; more than 40 countries and international organizations had signed cooperation agreements with China; Chinese companies had made over 50 billion USD of investment and launched a number of major projects in the countries along the routes, spurring the economic development of these countries and creating many local jobs.[15]

From May 14 to 15, 2017, the Belt and Road Forum for International Cooperation was held in Beijing. Over 1,500 representatives from more than 130 countries and over 70 international organizations attended the meeting, including 29 foreign heads of state, heads of government, and the UN Secretary-General and 2 other heads of important international organizations. President Xi Jinping said,

---

13   XI J P. Jointly compose a new and splendid chapter of the Silk Road: speech at the Legislative Chamber of the Supreme Assembly of Uzbekistan. People's Daily. 2016-06-23.
14   Sum up the experience, firm confidence, and promote the Belt and Road Initiative to benefit the peoples along the routes. People's Daily. 2016-08-18.
15   XI J P. Jointly shoulder responsibility of our times and promote global growth: keynote speech at the opening session of the World Economic Forum Annual Meeting 2017. People's Daily. 2017-01-18.

China will enhance friendship and cooperation with all countries involved in the Belt and Road Initiative on the basis of the Five Principles of Peaceful Coexistence. We are ready to share practices of development with other countries, but we have no intention to interfere in other countries' internal affairs, export our own social system and model of development, or impose our own will on others. In pursuing the Belt and Road Initiative, we will not resort to outdated geopolitical maneuvering. What we hope to achieve is a new model of win-win cooperation. We have no intention to form a small group detrimental to stability, what we hope to create is a big family of harmonious coexistence.[16]

Over the past four years, General Secretary Xi Jinping has expounded the Belt and Road Initiative many times, which makes it increasingly mature and consummate. In this process, the Belt and Road Initiative has been transformed from a macroscopic and abstract proposal of regional foreign policy into a comprehensive strategic concept, which both guides the medium and long-term economic and social development at home and serves as an external policy for building a community of shared future for mankind abroad. The Belt and Road Initiative is carried out steadily following General Secretary Xi Jinping's visits to foreign countries all over the globe. The Belt and Road Initiative has developed into an open international cooperation platform, which any like-minded countries can participate in, so that they will both benefit themselves and in turn promote the regional and world economic development by joining their development strategies with those of other countries and strengthening international cooperation.

2. The blueprint of the Belt and Road construction

The Belt and Road Initiative is hailed as the world's largest and most potential economic cooperation zone. The Asia-Europe continent is the main region covered by the Belt and Road Initiative, which run through the continents of Asia, Europe and Africa, connected the vibrant East Asia economic circle at one end and developed European economic circle at the other, and encompassed countries with huge potential for economic development.[17] The Silk Road Economic Belt is composed of three routes: the first

16   XI J P. Work together to build the Silk Road Economic Belt and the 21st Century Maritime Silk Road: speech at the opening ceremony of the Belt and Road Forum for International Cooperation. People's Daily. 2017-05-15.

17   Vision and actions on jointly building Silk Road Economic Belt and 21st Century Maritime Silk Road. Beijing: People's Publishing House. 2015: 6.

goes from China and extends westward to Central Asia, Russia and Europe (the Baltic); the second goes south westward, linking China with the Persian Gulf and the Mediterranean Sea through Central Asia and West Asia; and the third extends southward, connecting China with Southeast Asia, South Asia and the Indian Ocean. The 21st Century Maritime SilkRoad is made up of two routes: one is designed to go from China's coast to Europe through the South China Sea and the Indian Ocean, and the other from China's coast through the South China Sea to the South Pacific. The Belt and Road Initiative is characterized by ASEAN and Southeast Asian being the focus, driving South Asia, and radiating to the Middle East, East Africa and Europe. The land routes and the sea routes are joined up seamlessly, covering the new Eurasian Continental Bridge and such international economic cooperation corridors as the China-Mongolia-Russia Economic Corridor, the Central and the West Asian Economic Corridor, the Indo-China Peninsula Economic Corridor, the China-Pakistan Economic Corridor and the Bangladesh-China-India-Myanmar Economic Corridor. As a key partner in building the Belt and Road, Africa is closely linked with the Asia-Europe continent, and we should work together for common development. Oceania includes the southward extension of the 21st Century Maritime Silk Road. As an open platform, the Belt and Road Initiative also welcomes Latin American and Caribbean countries to participate in the construction. It also welcomes interested countries and international organizations to participate in different ways. China is also willing to work with the developed countries, to give to full play their complementary advantages in technology, capital, capacity and market, and carry out third-party cooperation in countries along the routes to promote mutual benefit and win-win result.

China believes that, to promote the Belt and Road Initiative, the overall idea is to "advocate peace and cooperation, openness and inclusiveness, mutual learning and mutual benefit. It promotes practical cooperation in all fields, and works to build a community of shared interests, destiny and responsibility featuring mutual political trust, economic integration and cultural inclusiveness."[18] Policy coordination, facilities connectivity, unimpeded trade, financial integration and people-to-people bonds are the core contents of the Belt and Road Initiative.

---

18 Vision and actions on Jointly Building Silk Road Economic Belt and 21st Century Maritime Silk Road. Beijing, People's Publishing House. 2015: 6.

First, enhancing policy coordination is an important guarantee for implementing the Initiative. "Countries should have full discussions on development strategies and policies, adopt plans and measures for advancing regional cooperation through consultation in the spirit of seeking common ground while reserving differences, and give the policy and legal' green light' to regional economic integration."[19]

Second, facilities connectivity is a priority area for implementing the Initiative. We will "open up a major transport route connecting the Pacific to the Baltic. On this basis, we can actively discuss the best way to improve cross-border transport infrastructure and work towards a transport network connecting East Asia, West Asia, and South Asia to facilitate economic development and travel in the region."[20]

Third, investment and trade cooperation is a major task in building the Belt and Road. The Belt and Road Initiative represents the biggest market in the world, with enormous and unparalleled potential for trade and investment cooperation between the countries involved. All participants should discuss a proper arrangement for trade and investment facilitation, remove trade barriers, reduce trade and investment costs, actively build free trade areas with the countries and regions along the routes, and stimulate the release of cooperation potential.

Fourth, financial integration is an important underpinning for implementing the Belt and Road Initiative. All parties concerned should deepen financial cooperation, and make more efforts in building a currency stability system, investment and financing system and credit information system in Asia. "If our region can realize local currency convertibility and settlement under the current and capital accounts, it will significantly lower circulation cost, increase our ability to fend off financial risks, and make our region more competitive internationally."[21] We should actively establish the AIIB, the NDB, the Silk Road Fund, SCO Development Bank and other financing institutions, and promote the development of financial cooperation. We should strengthen financial regulation, establish an efficient regulation coordination mechanism in the region, and build a regional financial risk early-warning system.

---

19   XI J P. The governance of China. Beijing: Foreign Languages Press. 2014: 289.
20   Ibid. 290.
21   XI J P. The governance of China. Beijing: Foreign Languages Press. 2014: 290.

Fifth, people-to-people bonds provide the public support for implementing the Initiative." Friendship between peoples is the key to good relations between states." We should carry forward the spirit of friendly cooperation of the Silk Road by promoting extensive cultural and academic exchanges, personnel exchanges and cooperation, media cooperation, youth and women exchanges and volunteer services, so as to win public support. Only when these five types of connectivity are all achieved, can we decide that the Belt and Road Initiative is successfully finished.

The Belt and Road Initiative and interconnection are closely related. They complement each other. "If we compare the Belt and Road to two wings for Asia's take-off, interconnection is the system of meridians on the two wings."[22] On November 8, 2014, President Xi Jinping stressed at the Dialogue on Strengthening Connectivity Partnership that China should consider Asian countries as a priority, economic corridors as the support pillars, transport infrastructure as the breakthrough, a financing platform as the mean and the people-to people bonds as the tie to boost the practical cooperation, deepen the interconnection and partnership between Asian countries, and build a community of shared destiny. He pointed out that interconnection is the pursuit of human society, and the Asian peoples can be called pioneers in building interconnection.

> The interconnection we need to build does not refer only to roads and bridges, or flat and single-line connection. Today's connectivity should be a three-way combination of infrastructure, institutions and people-to-people bonds and the progress in five areas of policy communication, infrastructure connectivity, trade link, capital flow, and understanding among people.[23]

The Belt and Road Initiative does not start from scratch, but is based on full use of existing bilateral and multilateral cooperation mechanisms. Metaphorically speaking, the "new wine" of the Belt and Road Initiative is filled into the "old bottle" of the existing mechanisms, to promote the participants' cooperation in the relevant key areas. In terms of bilateral cooperation, China actively promotes signing memoranda of understanding concerning the Belt and Road Initiative, or preparing bilateral cooperation

---

22   XI J P. Connectivity leads to development and partners focus on cooperation: speech at the dialogue on strengthening connectivity partnership. People's Daily. 2014-11-09.
23   XI J P. Connectivity leads to development and partners focus on cooperation: speech at the dialogue on strengthening connectivity partnership. People's Daily. 2014-11-09.

plans with the countries concerned, improves the bilateral working mechanism, and refines the Belt and Road Initiative and road map. Starting from this basis, we can promote the construction of a number of cooperative demonstration projects, so that the bilateral cooperation will run towards "the fast lane". In terms of multilateral cooperation, Chine should actively give full play to the SCO, China-ASEAN (10+1), APEC, Asia-Europe Meeting (ASEM), Asia Cooperation Dialogue (ACD), CICA, China-Arab States Cooperation Forum, China-GCC Strategic Dialogue, Greater Mekong Sub-region Economic Cooperation (GMS), Central Asia Regional Economic Cooperation (CAREC) and other existing multilateral cooperation mechanisms, so that more countries and regions can participate in the Belt and Road Initiative. We should give full play to the constructive role of the regional, sub regional international forums, trade shows, expos and other platforms of the countries along the routes. China is one of the pillars of the SCO. President Xi Jinping proposed,

> The SCO member states should intensify cooperation in energy and agriculture, speed up the construction of a platform for environmental-protection information, and ensure the success of the docking between the Silk Road Economic Belt and the Eurasian Economic Union, so as to promote a balanced development in the Eurasian region.[24]

ASEAN is the focus and the priority direction for China to implement the Belt and Road Initiative. The solid foundation laid by China-ASEAN dialogues and cooperation for more than 20 years is conducive to the implementation of the Belt and Road Initiative, enabling China and ASEAN to achieve a higher degree of interconnection and benign interaction. The Belt and Road Initiative has also stimulated the new vitality of APEC. "We need to take more vigorous action, realize the Free Trade Area of the Asia-Pacific (FTAAP) at an early date, and promote the open Asia-Pacific economy to a new height."[25]

The Belt and Road Initiative is not an empty slogan, but a series of real projects and measures taken to promote the docking of the development

---

24 XI J P. Unite and help each other and address challenges together to promote the SCO for New Leapfrog Progress: speech given at the 15th meeting of the Council of Heads of State of the Member States of the SCO. People's Daily. 2015-07-11.

25 XI J P. Forge ahead into the future for progress and prosperity in the Asia-Pacific: speech given at the 24th APEC Economic Leaders' Meeting the 24th APEC Economic Leaders' Meeting. People's Daily. 2016-11-22.

strategies of countries along the routes. It is not a Chinese version of the Marshall Plan, nor that of the Monroe Doctrine. The Marshall Plan was claimed to be an economic plan to aid Western Europe, yet its fundamental purpose lied in confrontation and competition for hegemony between the East and West. The Monroe Doctrine regarded Latin America as the US sphere of influence, therefore was essentially an embodiment of the US expansionism. The Belt and Road Initiative does not hold any country's development model and development path as a standard, but upholds the principle of mutual consultation, efforts and sharing, and promotes the Silk Road Spirit featuring peace and cooperation, openness and inclusiveness, mutual learning and mutual benefit. It benefits not only the Chinese people, but also the peoples of the participating countries, and promotes the overall prosperity and common progress of the world economy. As General Secretary Xi Jinping said, "the Belt and Road Initiative is not one party's private road but a bright path for all countries to join hands moving forward."[26]

3. Opportunities and challenges for the Belt and Road Initiative

The proposal and the implementation of the Belt and Road Initiative enjoy the advantages brought forward by good timing, geographical convenience and harmonious human relations. The so-called "good timing" refers that the world is undergoing complex and profound changes.

> The initiative to jointly build the Belt and Road is aimed at promoting orderly and free flow of economic factors, highly efficient allocation of resources and deep integration of markets; encouraging the countries along the Belt and Road to achieve economic policy coordination and carry out broader and more in-depth regional cooperation of higher standards; and jointly creating an open, inclusive and balanced regional economic cooperation architecture that benefits all.[27]

This initiative conforms to the world trends of multipolarization, economic globalization, cultural diversification and social informatization, which are in the fundamental interest of the international community. The

26   Xi Jinping attends and addresses the China-UK Business Summit. People's Daily. 2015-10-22.
27   Vision and actions on jointly building Silk Road Economic Belt and 21st Century Maritime Silk Road. Beijing: People's Publishing House. 2015: 3.

so-called "geographical convenience" refers to the foundation of the ancient Silk Road spiritual heritage and its rejuvenation. China is adjacent to countries along the Belt and Road in the vast hinter land on the Asia-Europe continent, and the all-round construction of the Belt and Road Initiative has unique geographical advantages. Asia today has become the world economic growth center, and there is strong economic complementarity among Asian countries. The success of China's economy has had a positive demonstration effect on many countries around the world, and the construction of the Belt and Road has a widespread appeal. The so-called "harmonious human relations" refers that the ancient Silk Road spread the outstanding achievements of Chinese civilization and the peaceful, open and inclusive concept of the Chinese nation. The ethnic minorities in China's northwest, southwest and other places, share the same ethnical and religious cultures, historical memories, customs and life styles with the countries and regions along the routes. The Belt and Road Initiative conveys not only such traditional ideas of peace in China as having faith and promoting good will and mutually offering support and assistance in times of adversity, but also the propositions of peaceful development and win-win cooperation, which will help to foster the sense of affinity and identity of the nations and peoples along the routes.

"The Belt and Road Initiative is a way for win-win cooperation that promotes common development and prosperity and a road towards peace and friendship by enhancing mutual understanding and trust, and strengthening all-round exchanges."[28] However, the construction process of the Belt and Road Initiative is still facing many real risks and challenges.

First, the global challenge posed by geopolitical game. Many areas along the Belt and Road have been battlegrounds since ancient times, and the geopolitical situations are unusually complicated and sensitive, the countries in these regions are strongly precautious. The interference and containment of strong powers out of the region are inevitable. For a long time, some neighboring countries of China took the dual profit strategy of "dependent on China for economic gains and on the United States for political interests," eying China with suspicion and mistrust in terms of political security. The Belt and Road Initiative gives priority to economy, making participating

---

28 Vision and actions on jointly building Silk Road Economic Belt and 21ˢᵗ Century Maritime Silk Road. Beijing: People's Publishing House. 2015: 5.

countries share the fruits of the China's economic growth. However, it arouses small and medium-sized countries' concerns, who are worried that they may become highly depend on China's economy, and that China's large-scale investment may change their own cultural traditions, and the like. To compete for geographical advantages and dominance, a small number of foreign powers outside the regions go still further to use such means as purposefully wooing small and medium sized countries and deliberately intensifying contradictions, to thwart the Belt and Road Initiative. A s President Xi Jinping put it, "to understand and appreciate a country with over 5,000 years of civilization, 56 ethnic groups and more than 1.3 billion people is no easy job. The most appropriate judgement should be based on facts, rather than glimpses through the fog."[29] The successful implementation of the Belt and Road Initiative depends on the strong support of the countries along the routes. China needs to take active measures to deal with the strategic cooperation with the participating countries that are in want of mutual trust, and fully mobilize the enthusiasm and sense of participation of the participating countries to reduce the resistance to the construction of the initiative.

Second, the political turmoil of some countries along the routes, and some normalized security threats. A number of countries along the Belt and Road are in transition, whose political ecology is likely to undergo sudden changes. On one hand, this situation distracts their elites' energy, which results in serious corruption, keeps their attention away from economic development and hinders their response to the needs of the Belt and Road construction; on the other hand, it may reduce the Belt and Road Initiative to a chip in their domestic political struggle or the object for them to shift their crises. At the same time, there are a large number of unresolved historical issues and racial and religious disputes, due to which regional conflicts are continuing, terrorism and religious extremism rampant, and piracies frequent. China is not optimistic about the security situation in the Central Asia, the West Asia and the North Africa. And terrorist activities have occurred in the Southeast Asia and the South Asia. This situation is not only a serious threat to the security of the personnel and facilities from both China and the participant countries in the Belt and Road Initiative, causing damage to the income and prospects of related project investments, but also to some

---

29   XI J P. Work together to promote openness, inclusiveness and peaceful development: speech at dinner hosted by the lord mayor of the city of London. People's Daily, 2015-10-23.

extent frustrates all parties' enthusiasm in the docking of their construction projects with the Belt and Road Initiative.

Third, the constraints from the internal separatist forces and sovereignty disputes. The separatist forces such as the "Tibet independence" and "Xinjiang independence" advocates have seriously harmed China's national unity and social stability. Despite being China's internal problems, the separatist activities of "Tibet independence" and "Xinjiang independence" are supported by foreign forces to varying degrees, and their long-term continuation is inseparable from the intervention of external forces. With the increase in the openness of the Belt and Road Initiative, the collusion and interaction between the internal separatist forces and foreign extremists, and between the ethnic separatists and the terrorists are possible to increase, posing threats to the internal and external safety that the Belt and Road Initiative efforts intended to achieve. In addition, there are still pending disputes over territorial and maritime rights around China. Some countries' provocative acts force China to use its actual actions to show its core interests and strategic bottom line, which, however, might intensify contradictions and exacerbate their vigilance, causing impact to the peaceful development environment necessary for the Belt and Road Initiative.

Fourth, the economic risks of the Belt and Road Initiative. Most of the economies along the routes are relatively underdeveloped. There are uncertain factors in their economic and social development; their overall investment environment is relatively poor, and the construction of their supporting mechanisms and facilities cannot fully meet the requirements of China's overseas investment for the time being. A large number of the Belt and Road construction projects focus on the field of infrastructure investment, with a long cycle of investment income and a rate of return on investment that we cannot be optimistic about. There is a general lack of adequate funding for the countries along the routes, and the financing pressure of the projects is enormous. The overseas investment of Chinese enterprises starts rather late, and is faced with entirely new social, economic, political and cultural environments. Therefore, it is inevitable for them to meet with problems of non-acclimatization in such aspects as production and management. And it is urgent for Chinese enterprises need to learn and adapt as soon as possible to the new environments, so as to avoid investment and operational risks.

The construction of the Belt and Road Initiative carries the mission of promoting the prosperity of the countries along the routes, strengthening the exchange and mutual learning of different civilizations and promoting the peaceful development of the world. Seen from the trends of the times, the historical and geographical endowment, the realistic demands and the aggregation of the people along the routes, the initiative is put forward exactly at the right time, and is full of opportunities. General Secretary Xi Jinping pointed out,

The Belt and Road Initiative can be seen as an opportunity to promote transnational interconnection, improve trade and investment cooperation, advance cooperation in international capacity and equipment manufacturing to rebalance and stabilize the world economy, which in essence is raising new demands by increasing effective supply. Especially against the backdrop of a sluggish global economy, our huge production capacity and building capacity formed in the pro-cyclical conditions can go out to support the countries along the routes, meet their urgent needs of promoting industrialization and modernization and improving the level of their infrastructure, and be conducive to stabilize the current world economy situation.[30]

Undoubtedly, opportunities and challenges always come together. The construction of the Belt and Road will inevitably see both risks and challenges. However, the sharing of opportunities as well as challenges is itself the guiding principle of the Belt and Road Initiative." Holding the spirit that self-confidence can empower a man to swim 3,000 miles and live for 200 years, we can fearlessly confront any challenge or difficulty that lies ahead, and resolutely open up new horizons and create new miracles."[31]

4. The progress and fruits of the Belt and Road Initiative

The Belt and Road Initiative received the attention, response, recognition and even creative expansion from all countries and international organizations in the world as soon as it was proposed. Over the past four years, the connotations, denotations and operation mechanisms of the Belt and Road Initiative have been continuously enriched and promoted. It has become a guiding principle for China's medium and long-term economic and social development, and an international cooperation platform for more and

30 Sum up the experience, firm confidence, and promote the Belt and Road Initiative to benefit the peoples along the routes. People's Daily. 2016-08-18.
31 XI J P. Speech at a Ceremony Marking the 15th Anniversary of the Founding of the Communist Party of China. Beijing: People's Publishing House. 2016: 12-13.

more countries. The construction of the Belt and Road has achieved more than expected results: the Belt and Road Initiative featuring peaceful cooperation, openness and inclusiveness, mutual learning, mutual benefit and win-win result; the initiative has long and successfully gone through the preparation and pioneering stages, and is now in the strategic implementation and the crucial stages. Over the past four years, the construction of the Belt and Road Initiative have been visually reflected in the statistical data. According to the data released by the State Council Information Office of the People's Republic of China, in 2016, while the international market demand continued to slump, China and the countries along the Belt and Road had a total import-export volume of 6.3 trillion CNY. As of 2016, Chinese enterprises had already built 56 economic cooperation zones in 20 countries along the Belt and Road, with a total investment of more than 18.5 billion USD, creating nearly 1.1 billion USD in taxes and 180,000 jobs for the host countries.[32] During 2014-2016, the total trade volume of China and countries along the routes was about 20 trillion CNY. In investment cooperation, the Chinese enterprises gave the countries along the routes direct investment of more than 50 billion USD, signed new contracts of foreign contracted projects with an amount of 301.9 billion USD with countries along the routes. The "circle of friends" of the Belt and Road Initiative has also been expanding. On May 10, 2017, the Office of the Leading Group for the Belt and Road Initiative released a report titled Constructing the Belt and Road: Concept, Practice and China's Contribution, which states that, as of the end of 2016, more than 100 countries have expressed their support and willingness to participate in the initiative. China has signed 46 cooperation agreements with 39 countries and international organizations, covering a broad range of fields that include connectivity, production capacity, investment, economy and trade, finance, science and technology, society, humanities, quality of life, and marine issues.

Over the past four years, the interconnection project has been an important part of the construction of the Belt and Road Initiative. It covers the "six means of communication", namely, rail, highways, seagoing transport, aviation, pipelines, and aerospace integrated information network, which comprise the main targets of infrastructure connectivity. Projects such as

---

32 The data is from for three consecutive years, consumption has become the first driving force (at the Press Conference of the State Council Information Office of the People's Republic of China). People's Daily. 2017-02-22.

the Sino-Myanmar railway, the Sino-Laos railway, the Sino-Thai railway, the Jakarta-Bandung High-speed Railway in Indonesia, the Chinese-Uzbekistan-Tajikistan railway, the Pan-Asia Railway Network, the China-Myanmar road and the China-Tajikistan road (Phase-IT) have made an early breakthrough. Projects such as the China-Myanmar Kyaukpyu Port special zone, the Sihanoukville Port Special Economic Zone Development Project and Sihanoukville Port Multi-Purpose Terminal Development Project, the Indonesian ports and Special Economic Zones, the Gwadar Port, the China-Central Asia Gas Pipelines A/B/C, the China Russia Oil Pipeline East Route and West Route have begun to bring in benefits. The Ethiopian Addis-Ababa-Djibouti Railway was opened to traffic. It is the first transnational electrified railway in Africa. Chinese enterprises have also participated in nearly 10 civil aviation infrastructure projects in more than 20 countries along the routes, and strived to achieve the skyward extension of the Belt and Road Initiative, making the Aerial Silk Road and the land and maritime routes add radiance and beauty to each other. China also cooperates with countries along the routes to promote cross-border optical cable communication network construction, promote the cooperation in the Internet, information technology, information economy and other areas, and improve the level of international communication interconnection.

Over the past four years, the financial support mechanism of the Belt and Road Initiative has begun to play a role. A total of nine projects were approved in the first year of the AIIB, with a total loan of approximately 1.7 billion USD, including the M4 Motorway project in Pakistan's Punjab province, the slum up grading project in Indonesia, and the Azerbaijan Trans-Anatolian Natural Gas Pipeline project. President Xi Jinping said,

> The demand for infrastructure development in Asia is enormous. Institutions for infrastructure investment, old or new, have much to offer each other, and may well work together through joint financing, knowledge sharing and capacity building. They may engage each other in benign competition, learn from and reinforce each other, and move forward in tandem. This is a way to allow multilateral development Institutions to Contribute more to infrastructure connectivity and sustainable economic development in the region.[33]

---

33   XI J P. Address at the AIIB Inauguration Ceremony. People's Daily. 2016-01-17.

As the investment and financing platform for the Belt and Road Initiative, the AIIB can solve the problem of misallocation of resources in the Asian region, realize the effective allocation of its savings and investment, and finance and invest in the world, to support the development of infrastructure in both Asia and other regions of the world. This will also improve the countries' investment environment along the Belt and Road. Through the investment and financing of the AIIB, we can achieve the cooperation between China and other countries, promote the strategic transfer of industrial capacity, and create a new industrial chain of international trade, to promote the better and faster development of the Belt and Road Initiative. At present, in terms of the size of the member countries, the AIIB has become second only to the World Bank as a global multilateral development agency, exceeding the scale of both the European Bank for Reconstruction and Development and the Asian Development Bank. After its establishment, according to the principles of "marketization, internationalization and specialization," the Silk Road Fund focuses on supporting the development of real economy and actively promoting the investment of large-scale projects with driving forces of economic development. At the end of 2016, Silk Road Fund has signed 15 projects covering Russia, Mongolia, Central Asia, South Asia, Southeast Asia and other countries and regions, and committed to the cumulative investment of about 6 billion USD.

Over the past four years, the construction of international economic corridors within the framework of the Belt and Road Initiative has achieved significant results. The Bangladesh-China-India-Myanmar Economic Corridor, based on the existing civil economic and academic exchanges in the region, was jointly proposed by the China and India in May 2013, and received positive responses from Bangladesh and Myanmar. In December 2013, the first meeting of the Bangladesh-China-India-Myanmar Economic Corridor Joint Working Group was held in Kunming. The parties signed the meeting minutes and the Bangladesh-China-India-Myanmar Economic Corridor Joint Research Program, formally established the mechanism for the four governments to promote cooperation, with the aim to set up a corn prehensive strategic channel of traffic, energy, trade logistics, industrial cooperation, cultural exchanges and other functions. The second meeting of the Working Group in 2014 discussed the priorities and direction of the development of the Bangladesh-China-India-Myanmar Economic Corridor.

The China-Pakistan Economic Corridor is the key link connecting the sea and land routes, and running through the north and south Silk Roads.

The China-Pakistan Economic Corridor is a focal point of our joint efforts to achieve common development, and we should use this economic corridor to drive our practical cooperation with focus on Gwadar Port, energy, infrastructure development and industrial cooperation, and establish a "1+4" cooperation layout.[34]

In April 2015, the China-Pakistan Economic Corridor Commission was formally established. On May 13, 2015, Gwadar port officially opened to use. On May 21, 2015, the equipment contract of Pakistan Port Qasim 1320 Megawatts Thermal Power Project was signed, officially launching the first energy project in the China-Pakistan Economic Corridor. On April 1, 2017, the Pakistan Dawood Wind Power Project officially started commercial operation, which was the first energy project to achieve commercial operation in the China-Pakistan Economy Corridor.

The construction of the China-Mongolia-Russia Economic Corridor was initiated in September 2014, when President Xi Jinping attended the first Meeting of the Three Heads of State of China, Russia and Mongolia. He said, "we can link the Silk Road Economic Belt with Russia's initiative of the Railway across Eurasia and Mongolia's initiative of the Prairie Road, forge the China-Mongolia-Russia Economic Corridor, strengthen connectivity construction of highways and railways, promote the facilitation of customs clearance and transport, promote cooperation in transit transport, carry out research on construction of trilateral cross-border transmission grid, and conduct practical cooperation in tourism, think tank, media, environmental protection, disaster mitigation and relief and other fields."[35] In September 2016, the Plan on Establishing the China-Mongolia-Russia Economic Corridor was released, which clarified the specific contents, sources of funds and implementation mechanism of the economic corridor, and agreed on 32 key cooperation projects, covering ten key areas, marking the formal start of the economy corridor construction.

---

34   XI J P. Building a China-Pakistan community of shared destiny to pursue closer win-win cooperation: speech at the Parliament of Pakistan. People's Daily. 2015-04-22.
35   Xi Jinping attends Meeting of the Three Heads of State of China, Russia and Mongolia. People's Daily. 2014-09-12.

The construction of the new Eurasian Continental Bridge Economic Corridor is based on modern international logistics systems such as China Railway Express, focusing on the development of economic, trade and production cooperation and expanding the cooperation space for energy resources. By the end of 2016, the operating China Railway Express service lines were up to 39, with a total of nearly 3,000 trains, covering 14 cities in 9 European countries, serving as an important platform for countries along the routes to promote connectivity and enhance the level of economic and trade cooperation.

Over the past four years, the cultural and people-to-people exchanges between China and the countries along the routes have become even closer. The Belt and Road Initiative inherits thousands of years of friendly exchange tradition along the Silk Road and gives it new meanings of the new era, so that the Chinese Dream will be integrated with the dreams of the peoples along the routes. There are a wide range of cultural and people-to-people communication and a variety of contents in the Belt and Road Initiative. The Chinese government has signed intergovernmental cultural and people-to-people exchange agreements with most of the countries along the routes, and there are frequent inter-governmental visits and active non-governmental exchanges. Education exchange years, cultural tourism years, international expositions, film festivals and other activities provide various forms of platforms. People-to-people exchange is the basis of public opinion of the Belt and Road Initiative. Friendship between peoples is the key to good relations between states. Understanding each other is the key to the friendship between peoples. At the Dialogue on Strengthening Connectivity Partnership held in November 2014, President Xi Jinping proposed to "make human communication as a link, and consolidate the social basis for Asian connectivity,"[36] and announced to offer 20,000 training opportunities in China for connectivity professionals from neighboring countries in the next five years, in a bid to promote people-to-people exchanges. China has also set up Silk Road scholarships and government scholarships to support 10, 000 new students from countries along the routes to pursue studies or researches in China each year. In March 2011, the Silk Road Film and Television Bridge was kicked off, which enabled China and countries

---

36 XI J P. Connectivity leads to development and partners focus on cooperation: speech at the dialogue on strengthening connectivity partnership. People's Daily. 2014-11-09.

along the routes to jointly launch movies, TV dramas and documentaries with the subject matter of the Belt and Road Initiative. In June 2011, China, Kazakhstan and Kyrgyzstan formally launched the project to apply for adding the Silk Road on to the UNESCO World Heritage List, and the Silk Road was successfully included into it. In December 2014, the Silk Road Book Project organized and implemented by the State Administration of Press, Radio, Film and Television of the People's Republic of China was started. In April 2016, the application for adding the Maritime Silk Road onto the UNESCO World Cultural Heritages List was officially launched. As of the end of 2016, China has set up 30 Chinese cultural centers in countries along the Belt and Road, newly built a number of Confucius Institutes, and begun to hold the Silk Road International Cultural Expos, Silk Road International Arts Festivals, Maritime Silk Road International Arts Festivals and other activities. The Belt and Road cultural and people-to-people cooperation has achieved positive results, and filled a lasting vitality into the political mutual trust and the deepening of economic and trade cooperation.

5. The significance of constructing the Belt and Road

The Belt and Road Initiative is a major strategic decision made by the leadership of the CPC Central Committee with Comrade Xi Jinping as the core under the new historical conditions in implementing the all-round opening up and the over-all planning of both domestic and international situations. It is a major theoretical innovation of major-country diplomacy with Chinese characteristics. By this initiative, the Chinese Dream of the great rejuvenation of the Chinese nation is linked to the wonderful dreams of the peoples all over the world in pursuit of development and prosperity and has far reaching strategic significance.

The Belt and Road Initiative sets building a community of shared future for mankind as its goal, breaks the historical logic that a country will definitely seek hegemony when it grows stronger, and makes theoretical innovations in the traditional national development strategy. As an enormous inclusive development platform, the Belt and Road Initiative abides by the purposes and principles of the UN Charter, adheres to the principles of openness and cooperation, harmony and inclusiveness, market operation, mutual benefit and win-win result, and mutual efforts. It completely abandons the zero-sum mentality and sense of hegemony long pursued by Western countries in their development, and embodies the innovative thinking of major-country diplomacy with Chinese characteristics. China has benefited from the international community in its development process and is willing to contribute to the development of the international community with its own development. The interaction between China and the world is becoming closer and closer, and their opportunity and future sharing relationship has become increasingly prominent. In essence, the Belt and Road Initiative is a new model of international political and economic cooperation as well as the road leading to a community of shared future for mankind. It uses economic cooperation as the guide, political cooperation as the promoter, people-to-people exchange as the basis, integrates the domestic development strategy with the international strategy, and harmonizes China's interests and other countries' interest demands. With a Chinese philosophy of "being righteous alone in a community where the general moral tone is low when you are nobody, and benefit all peoples under the sky when you are somebody," the Belt and Road Initiative strives to build a grand blueprint for both China and the countries along the routes and even all countries in the world to jointly realize their dreams and pursue their happy future. The construction of the Belt and Road is committed to exploring a new type of international relations featuring win-win cooperation and embodying the concept of win-win cooperation in various aspects of international cooperation including the political, economic, security, civilization, ecological aspects, with important constructive significances for future international relations. The Belt and Road Initiative provides a new space for the China's sustainable economic development, mobilizes and integrates both international and domestic resources, and builds a new all-round open architecture.

To be confidently open to the outside world, a country must be strong enough, and being open to the outside world promotes a countries strength. The achievements of China's reform and opening up since the Third Plenary Session of the 11th CPC Central Committee have fully proved that opening to the outside world is an important driving force for China's economic and social development. With our economic output ranking second in the world, as China's economic development enters in to the new normal, to maintain sustained and healthy economic development, we must establish a global perspective, more consciously coordinate the domestic and international situations, comprehensively plan the grand strategy of all-round opening up, and goes to the world with a more active attitude.[37]

Due to the differences in the physical and geographical environments and the social environments between China's eastern and western parts, the Chinese economy as a whole shows a pattern of unbalanced development that features a faster eastern part and a slower western part, as well as a stronger coastland and a weaker hinterland. The Belt and Road stretch across the eastern, central and western regions of China. While increasing the level of opening up of the east, the initiative focuses on increasing the degree of opening of the central and western regions, so as to optimize the utilization of regional resources, open the international market channels for the central and western regions, cultivate the international market space, and turn the hinterland into an open frontier. The construction of the Belt and Road gives full play to the comparative advantages of all regions in China, promotes the orderly free flow of the economic elements and the highly efficient allocation of production resources, so as to achieve the docking of the eastern coastal areas and the central and the western regions, to create a comprehensive, multi-angle and deep level framework of opening to the outside world, to balance the eastern and western social and economic development, and to promote the overall development level and quality of the Chinese society.

The construction of the Belt and Road will accelerate the integration of China's economy with the world economy, providing new opportunities for the world's economic development. General Secretary Xi Jinping remarked,

> Rapid growth in China has been a sustained, powerful engine for global economic stability and expansion. The inter-connected development of China and a large number of other countries has made the world economy more balanced. China's remarkable achievement in poverty reduction has contributed to more inclusive global growth. And China's continuous progress in reform and opening-up has lent much momentum to an open world economy.[38]

---

37   Sum up the experience, firm confidence, and promote the Belt and Road Initiative to benefit the peoples along the routes. People's Daily. 2016-08-18.
38   XI J P. Jointly shoulder responsibility of our times, promote global growth: keynote speech at the opening session of the World Economic Forum Annual Meeting 2017. People's Daily. 2017-01-18.

The construction of the Belt and Road provides a more convenient channel for countries along the routes to participate in the development of the Chinese market, to share the achievements and experience of China's economic development, to promote the efficient allocation of resources and economic policy coordination of the participating countries, to achieve a wider range, higher level and deeper layer of international cooperation, and take the path of common construction, common development and common prosperity. With the gradual implementation of the Belt and Road Initiative, the international community is generally aware of this historic opportunity. Many countries respond positively and take the initiative to seek the strategic docking of their own development strategy and the Belt and Road Initiative, in the hope of gaining momentum from this initiative to their own development or their regional development. The Belt and Road Initiative "focuses on the Asian, European and African continents, but is also open to all other countries. All countries, from either Asia, Europe, Africa or the Americas, can be international cooperation partners of the Belt and Road Initiative."[39] At present, China has signed memoranda of understanding with Hungary, Tajikistan, Kazakhstan, Qatar, Kuwait and other countries to construct the Belt and Road. In April 2016, China and the UN Economic and Social Commission for Asia and the Pacific signed the Letter of Intent Between Ministry of Foreign Affairs of the People's Republic of China and the U N Economic and Social Commission for Asia and the Pacific on Advancing Regional Connectivity and the Belt and Road Initiative, which is the first document on cooperation inbuilding the Belt and Road Initiative between China and an international organization. In March 2017, China and the New Zealand signed Belt and Road cooperation agreement, which made the New Zealand the first Western developed country to sign a relevant agreement.

The Belt and Road Initiative fully demonstrates China's will, capability and wisdom to participate in global governance and shape the international order, and effectively enhances China's international influence and voice. The countries and regions along the routes are an important area of overseas interests of China's concern. Implementation of the Belt and Road

---

39 XI J P. Work together to build the Silk Road Economic Belt and the 21ˢᵗ Century Maritime Silk Road: speech at the Opening Ceremony of the Belt and Road Forum for International Cooperation. People's Daily. 2017-05-15.

Initiative helps to effectively protect China's growing overseas interests, increase China's weight in the neighborhood and international affairs. The Belt and Road Initiative is not only an economic blueprint, but also a deeper level of peace concept, security consensus and cultural values. It conveys to the world China's concepts of peace, development, win-win cooperation, and manifests the self-confidence in its socialist path, theory, institution and culture with Chinese characteristic. It is conducive to stabilize China's surrounding geopolitical environment, and provides a new platform for China's all-round diplomacy, so that China, together with countries along the routes and participants in the Belt and Road Initiative, is able to provide new international public goods in the reform of the global governance system. To China,

> With the lofty cause of peace and development of the world in mind, we will contribute the Chinese vision to the management of contemporary international relations, offer the Chinese solution for improving global governance, and work with the international society to meet various challenges of the 21st century.[40]

In March 2016, the UN Security Council adopted Resolution 2274 on Afghanistan, which for the first time, includes contents of the implementation of the Belt and Road Initiative. In November 2016, the 71st Session of the General Assembly, by consensus, adopted Resolution A/71/9 on Afghanistan and welcomed the assistance provided to Afghanistan by the Belt and Road Initiative. This is the first time for the Belt and Road Initiative to be included in a UN General Assembly resolution, which reflects the universal recognition of the international community to implement the Belt and Road Initiative. In March 2017, the Security Council unanimously adopted Resolution 2344 on Afghanistan, calling on the international community to gather consensus on assistance to the Afghans, strengthen regional economic cooperation through the Belt and Road Initiative, and urge all parties to provide security for the construction of the Belt and Road, to strengthen the strategy docking of their development policies, to promote connectivity and pragmatic cooperation, and so on. The discourse system with Chinese characteristics began to be better understood and accepted by the international community and other countries.

---

40   XI J P. Speech at the Körber Foundation, Germany. People's Daily. 2014-03-20.

As the Chinese old saying goes, "One who does not consider the issue from the perspective of long-term interests can rarely be able to plan well; one who does not consider the overall interests as an issue can barely be able to plan well." Though the good vision of construction of the Belt and Road seems to be too far away to reach, "the fruits of the Initiative will benefit the whole world. They both serve as a driving force to China, and create opportunities for the world. China is willing to work with like-minded countries in the 'nail-driving spirit', and steadfastly push forward the Belt and Road Initiative step by step."[41]

Since the 18th CPC National Congress, Xi Jinping's diplomatic thought has been developing continuously and perfected in the diplomatic practice of major-country relations with Chinese characteristic by forming a complete scientific system. This system has rich essence of Chinese traditional culture and reflects the trends of the times. At present, the international community is in the transitional period of great changes. It is strongly hoped that statesmen can step forward bravely, and the responsible major countries can provide solutions to the global issues. Xi Jinping's diplomatic thought sets the achievement of the Chinese Dream of the great rejuvenation of the Chinese nation and a community of shared future for mankind as the goals, holds high the banner of peace, development, cooperation and win-win result, firmly sticks to the path of peaceful development, promotes the sound values of friendship, justice and shared interests, strives to forge a new type of international relations featuring win-win cooperation, and demonstrates to the world China's political commitment and brilliant wisdom as a responsible major country. In the face of the historical changes in the balance of power in international relations, General Secretary Xi Jinping, with the overall strategic thinking and the active and enterprising spirit of innovation, made a farsighted Chinese initiative to lead the global governance system reform, and proposed to the world the Chinese framework of the Belt and Road Initiative, drawing a new blueprint for the development and progress of the international community. His diplomatic thought has written a new chapter in Chinese diplomatic theory, and opened up a new situation for Chinese diplomatic practice. It will surely continue to guide Chinese diplomacy to make greater contribution to the realization of the Chinese Dream of the great renewal of the Chinese nation, and promote the great process of building a community of shared future for mankind.

---

41 Sum up the experience, firm confidence, and promote the Belt and Road Initiative to benefit the peoples along the routes. People's Daily. 2016-08-18.